Every Day Magic
– A Pagan Book
of Days

366 Magical Ways to Observe the Cycle
of the Year

Every Day Magic – A Pagan Book of Days

366 Magical Ways to Observe the Cycle
of the Year

Edited by Lucya Starza

Winchester, UK
Washington, USA

First published by Moon Books, 2017
Moon Books is an imprint of John Hunt Publishing Ltd., Laurel House, Station Approach,
Alresford, Hants, SO24 9JH, UK
office1@jhpbooks.net
www.johnhuntpublishing.com
www.moon-books.net

For distributor details and how to order please visit the 'Ordering' section on our website.

Text copyright: Lucya Starza 2016

ISBN: 978 1 78535 567 7
978 1 78535 568 4 (ebook)
Library of Congress Control Number: 2016963554

A CIP catalogue record for this book is available from the British Library.

Design: Stuart Davies

Printed and bound by CPI Group (UK) Ltd, Croydon, CR0 4YY, UK

We operate a distinctive and ethical publishing philosophy in all
areas of our business, from our global network of authors to
production and worldwide distribution.

CONTENTS

Many thanks to Trevor Greenfield for his support as publisher at Moon Books, John Davies for proofreading, Paula Dempsey for her advice on astrology and help with writing the introductions to each month, and the artist Carl Newman for letting me photograph one of his beautiful hare brooches as part of my front cover collage.

Foreword by Trevor Greenfield

As the publisher of Moon Books it is my pleasant task to welcome *Every Day Magic – A Pagan Book of Days* into the Moon Books catalogue, to thank each of the contributors for their efforts and for sharing their knowledge and wisdom, and to congratulate Lucya Starza on the extraordinary achievement of bringing together writers from across the globe and organizing their work into a book that offers a treasure trove of ideas and information.

From a Moon Books perspective, *Every Day Magic* is not just another Pagan title. When we started Moon Books, more than five years ago, one of the critical success factors for us would be the extent to which we were able to engender a community of authors, both those writing best-sellers and those who wished to offer contributions to anthologies, who at times would come together and produce books exactly like this...a book authored by the Moon Books community of writers for the Moon Books community of readers.

Every Day Magic is designed to be read and reread. It is a book for the discerning shelf, to be referenced many times over many years. So here it is, a celebration of the Pagan traditions spread out across the year. May every reading be a blessing...

Trevor Greenfield

Introduction

Every Day Magic – A Pagan Book of Days contains 366 spells, rituals, meditations, Pagan prayers, divinatory techniques, poems to read and recipes and craft projects to try out along with the details of festivals that take place throughout the year. All the activities are intended to be easy to follow so you can just pick up the book, open it to a day and find something you can do. There are festivals from the ancient world and modern Pagan celebrations as well as other annual events with a Pagan or shamanic feel, such as Earth Day on April 22.

The book is a compilation of contributions from the Moon Books community of authors and writers, giving an insight into different traditions and how each day of the month throughout the cycle of the seasons can be celebrated.

Contributors came from all over the world and so I have left spellings and measurements in the style each individual wrote them. For a book that seems like a magical cabinet of curiosities, to be opened and perused with delight at the variety within, it would have felt wrong to try to make all the entries homogenous. The internet is out there and it is easy to find equivalent measurements for cups, litres, inches or centimetres. Editing this book has been a delight and I have learnt a great deal from reading all the entries. I have also enjoyed writing for it myself and sharing my own perspective on English witchcraft and candle magic.

Although each entry is listed for a specific day, obviously there are differences in the times when seasonal activities are appropriate depending on your location or variations in weather from one year to the next. Use the book as a guide, but feel free to do the spells and other activities whenever you want or whenever feels right for where you live. If a plant or animal mentioned cannot be found in your part of the world, then research an equivalent or simply visualise it in your mind's eye. I should add that most of the entries were written for the northern hemisphere. My only regret is that the book could not be big enough to give seasonally appropriate alternatives for the southern hemisphere as well. Perhaps there will be a future edition for the southern hemisphere too.

Every Day Magic – A Pagan Book of Days is a perennial book, designed to be used this year, next year and for as long as you follow the Pagan path. With it you will never be short of inspiration for ways to honour nature, the ancient Gods and Goddesses, those who went before us and the spirits of the places we live in now. Dip into it occasionally, or read it every day. If you want to find out more about any of the activities, in the last chapter – About the Contributors – there are details of the authors and their other books, blogs and websites. This means you can use *Every Day Magic – A Pagan Book of Days* as a starting-off point for further magical and spiritual exploration.

Lucya Starza

January

Often the coldest month of the year in the northern hemisphere, January can be bleak. The Moon in January is sometimes called Wolf Moon, Ice Moon, or Quiet Moon. It evokes the image of a wolf howling at the full Moon in a snow-covered landscape on an otherwise silent night. However, the days are noticeably starting to get longer, offering hope for the year ahead even as we brace ourselves against the chill outside or spend time indoors by a warming fire, kindling our hopes and dreams for the future.

In astrology, much of the month is ruled by Capricorn, which the Sun entered at the Winter Solstice. The symbol of a mountain goat with the tail of a fish is based on the Sumerian God of wisdom and waters, Enki. The fish-tailed goat is a versatile, tough creature that embodies the ability to push on with ambitions despite hostile environments. Despite its wise and watery origins, Capricorn is a materialistic sign and those born under it tend to associate material success with personal feelings of security. The Sun in Capricorn can lend power to spells for material goals, even if those goals will be hard to achieve. The Sun enters Aquarius on or around January 20, softening Capricorn's materialism. Aquarians are still acquisitive, but not at any cost. The water carrier is the sign of thoughts and new ideas, further helping us to plan for the year ahead. Use this in magic to empower your New Year's resolutions.

1. New Year's Resolutions: Resolve to enrich your spirit each and every day in many and varied ways. Aim to watch the way the seasons change; meditate a little; whisper prayers; light candles for peace, hope, joy, love and good health; dance and sing; learn about the Gods and Goddesses of the ancient world and celebrate the forces of nature, the Earth, the Sun, the Moon and the stars. Breathe in love and breathe out love. Be open to inspiration. Be blessed. *Lucya Starza*

2. Kakizome: This is the first calligraphy writing of the year in Japan. Make a wish or charm for what you hope the year will bring. Create a simple poem containing words that echo your wishes. Write it in decorative script and add elaborate decoration as a border around the words. Slowly read your words and wishes. Then burn the paper in a cauldron and release the charm to the elements. Toast the future in sake or wine. *Rachel Mayatt*

3. Think More, Act Later: In the northern hemisphere, people are just becoming aware of the small growing spark of light of the returning Sun. Think about what you would like to grow in your life this year. Is there a personal goal that you would like to accomplish? Do you want to spend more time with your family and/or friends or less time? Now is the time to think about it, not do it, because it is the wrong time for doing, that time is Imbolc (February 1), which is why New Year's resolutions often fail. *Brendan Howlin*

4. Janus: January is named after the Roman God of beginnings and endings, Janus. At the start of the year, cakes made of spelt flour and salt were traditionally burnt on his altar as an offering. Bake spelt bread (there are many traditional recipes online), then make an offering of a little to Janus. Tell him all the things you want to change and ask for his help. Light a candle in his honour. *Ravenwings*

5. Focus and Control Pouch:

Braided string, 6 inches in black, blue and yellow
Almond
Cedar
Bay leaf

Nutmeg
Carnelian
Cinnamon oil
Pouch
Purple candle

Before preparing the pouch, apply cinnamon oil to the candle. Light it to aid focus and meditation. Leaving the oil on your hands, continue the work. Affirmation: *'I am strong. I will focus. I remain calm, and use wisdom.'* Repeat this as you place the rest of the items into the pouch. Tie it with braided string. **Laeynarrie Auvresti**

6. Twelfth Night Wassail: Recite this to an apple tree and offer it cider and toast:

Wassail
Old Apple tree, old apple tree,
We have come to wassail thee.
Thirteen fires we bring to thee,
Ancient Mother apple tree.
Here's cider-toast to break thy fast,
Now winter lessens here at last.
We wake the spirits with the gun,
Then sing and dance, have lots of fun.
Oh apple tree, oh apple tree,
Do blossom well we beg o' thee.
To bear and to bow apples enow.
Hats full! Caps full! Three bushel bags full!
Barn floors full,
And a little heap under the stairs.
Elen Sentier

7. Distaff Day: This is the traditional date for women to return to household chores after the Christmas celebrations. Symbolically sweep all the dust and debris out of the house to begin a fresh start to the New Year. *Mélusine Draco*

8. Roman Feast Day of Justitia, Goddess of Justice: This is a good day for spells for the successful outcome of any legal matters or situations where justice is needed. Burn a purple candle and ask Justitia for justice. *Mélusine Draco*

9. Agonalia: Roman feast day of Priapus, a fertility God and protector of livestock, gardens and male genitalia. He was renowned for having a huge penis and statues of him depict this. It is also a good day for giving blessings on the threshold of your house so no ill-fortune will enter. *Mélusine Draco*

10. Sacred Bath: Rather than trying to battle away the shadows of January, spend time nurturing yourself. Here is a recipe for a soothing, sacred bath. Salt is a deep cleanser on an energetic level, and also good for aching muscles. Take one cup of sea salt and half a cup of Epsom salts. Mix them together while picturing your soothing intent. Then add six drops each of rose and lavender essential oils. Mix well and add a cupful to a warm bath. *Rebecca Beattie*

11. Old New Year: Today is a fire festival celebrated as Old New Year after historic calendar reforms and also the Feast of Juturna, Roman Goddess of fountains and the underworld, whose symbol is the spring. Celebrate a true Pagan New Year according to the Old Ways with plenty of good food and wine. Hold a private New Year celebration for Pagan friends only. By the light of a small bonfire let each guest pour a libation of wine into the flames while silently making a wish for the coming year. *Mélusine Draco*

12. Poem for the Day:

Winter
Grey sky,
turning to black.
Running for cover;
I am not a duck.

Pets gather,
at the heater.
Electric blanket
is a life-saver.

Wind;
cold, wet
and incessant.
I am still not
a bloody duck!

Hibernatingů.
Ronin Shaman

13. Tjugondagen Knut: On Tjugondagen Knut, Swedes, Finns and Norwegians strip their Christmas tree of cookies and boiled sweets (the traditional decorations) and cast the tree out. This is also called 'julgransplundring' (plundering the Christmas tree). On St Knut's Day people used to dress up as scarecrows, hags or straw goats and knock on doors scaring people. Hang cookies and sweets in your Christmas tree this year. Invite children over on St Knut's Day to plunder the tree – they will love it! *Imelda Almqvist*

14. Spell to Let Go: You need a piece of string, a burning bowl and a lighter. Winter is a good time to prepare the ground for spring. Sit quietly, centre and ground yourself. Ask yourself what you can let go of and whatever floats into your awareness, blow this into the string and tie a knot. When finished hold the string over the burning bowl and light it, letting it fall into the bowl and burn away. Scatter the ashes in the wind. *Yvonne Ryves*

15. The Minotaur: What's at the center of the Labyrinth? Not a monster, but your own Shadow Self. Take a few minutes to own your darkness. Breathe deeply into your anger, your frustration, your sadness. These are a part of you just as much as the light. Honor your darkness. Ask the Minotaur to help you draw strength from the shadows and understand that you are a whole being. All of you is valuable and worthy. *Laura Perry*

16. Altar to Invite Harmony Throughout the Year: The Roman Goddess Concordia is a gentle, kind Goddess who has acute ability in mediation. On this day in 10CE, Emperor Tiberius rededicated her temple. Create an altar to Concordia to invite peaceful exchanges throughout the year. Her sacred objects are the olive branch, the cornucopia (horn of plenty), and the patera (sacrificial bowl) from which libations are poured. The stork and dove are her companions. *Tiffany Lazic*

17. Old Twelfth Night: Honour the Lady with these words:

Mari Llwyd
Lady of Winter, Bride of Spring,
We know the light is coming in.
Come round the village with us now,
Fetch out the folk and make a row.
Tease them, riddle them, wake them up,
For summer's coming, with all luck.
Dance with us, Rhiannon's horse,
And let the seasons run their course.

We wake thee up, as every year,
To show us all there's nowt to fear
In darkness, cold and winter night,
For they're but harbingers of light.
Elen Sentier

18. Sunstone: We all struggle in January, Yule feels like months ago, but the dark, cold and rain persist. To help you through the dark, place a piece of sunstone in a sunny spot to get a full day's charge in the Sun. It will then carry the Sun's energy within. Carry it with you to keep the January blues at bay. You may find it helpful to have a couple of pieces to swap out while each other is charging. *Jenny Cartledge*

19. Ancient Egyptian Festival of Neith, Goddess of the Hunt and Warfare: Make an offering to end discord in the world. This could be a ritual offering by burning incense or pouring a libation of wine, it could be a financial offering of money to a charity that helps with peaceful resolutions of disputes, or you could volunteer time to work for peace and harmony in the world. *Mélusine Draco*

20. Baba Yaga Day: Baba in Slavic means 'old woman' and thus Baba Yaga is associated with the Crone. Baba Yaga is depicted as an old hag who lives in the deep woods in a hut surrounded by a fence of human bones and skulls. She is dark, rude, crude and shrewd. Her frightening exterior hides her inner beauty. It is said she guards the waters of life and death. Celebrate the wisdom and beauty of the Crone. Phone or visit an elderly neighbour or relative. *Morgana Phenix*

21. First Day of Luis (Rowan) Month in the Celtic Tree Calendar: The Celtic Tree calendar is a 13-month calendar based on 28-day months. Rowan is the second of the months and lasts from 21 January to the 17 February. One of rowan's uses is to repel dark spirits. It is used as a protector of people, land and livestock. Find a friendly rowan and ask if it would be happy to gift you a piece of itself either to carry on your person or to adorn a doorway to protect you and your home. *Jo Robson*

22. Feast of St Vincent in the Old Agricultural Calendar: The weather on this day was used as a forecast: wind and sunshine were favourable omens for the coming year's crops and grain. Go outside, see what the weather is like and make your own prediction. *Mélusine Draco*

23. Knot Magic: Traditionally, Cornish witches would create wind knots for sailors – three knots in a rope. Sailors would later untie the knots to release the wind: one for a fair wind, two for strong wind, three for a gale. But you can use knot magic for anything you want to wish for. Tie three knots in a rope and say:

Knot 1: My spell begun
Knot 2: My wish come true
Knot 3: So mote it be
Lucya Starza

24. Pendulum Dowsing to Find Lost Things: Sometimes called divining, this is traditionally used to find water below ground, but you can dowse to find mislaid objects. Hold the pendulum by its chain or cord and concentrate on what you are looking for. It should swing in the direction you need to go. Triangulate using the pendulum in several places to see where the lines converge. If you are over the thing you want, it should go round in a circle rather than swing backwards and forwards. *Lucya Starza*

25. Burns Night: This commemorates the life of Scottish poet Robert Burns, the Bard of Ayrshire. Inspired poetry can be a great way to tune in to your inner self. Calm your mind then read something aloud in a language you do not speak or tune a radio to a foreign station. Focus on the sounds. Don't think about meaning, just note down any words that you are reminded of. Once you have your words, think about the message they convey and what that means for you. *Carol Tierney*

26. Beat the January Blues: Wrap up warm, get outside and go for a walk in nature or in your local park to make the most of the daylight – even if that is just in your lunch hour. Make a donation to charity, even a very small one. In the evening, light a candle and meditate on its bright flame. *Lucya Starza*

27. Feast Day of Thoth, the Magician's Magician: Make an offering to Thoth, the Ancient Egyptian God of magic, to increase your magical powers. A suitable offering could be frankincense incense or essential oil. *Mélusine Draco*

28. Poem for the Day:

Witch
Wise woman
of the hedge.

Stir and chant,
magic from plants.

Midwife and healer,
black cat familiar

Chased away
by the cross.
Ronin Shaman

29. Charge Candles by Moonlight: On the night of a full Moon close to Imbolc (February 1) gather unused candles that you might later want to use for spells, rituals or votive lights. Hold them up to the light of the full Moon and say:

May these candles be cleansed by the light of the moon.
May these candles be blessed by the light of the moon.
May these candle be charged by the light of the moon!

Leave the candles on your windowsill or outdoors where they will be bathed in moonlight. **Lucya Starza**

30. Imbolc Potato Chowder:

1 large onion, chopped
2 tbsp vegan butter
2 tsp garlic powder
3 tbsp vegetable bouillon paste
4 lbs potatoes, peeled and chopped
5 cups unsweetened almond milk
2 tbsp parsley
4 tbsp nutritional yeast (cheese substitute)
2 tsp dried dill
½ cup instant mashed potato

Sauté the onion in butter until translucent. Add the other ingredients except the instant potato, simmer until potatoes are tender and beginning to lose shape. Add the instant mashed potato, stir to thicken. Simmer for 10 more minutes. *Amie Ravenson*

31. A Day of Hecate: Hecate, keeper of the crossroads, is a Goddess of great power and strength. You can call on her when you're faced with a difficult decision. Create an altar, including keys and candles to represent her torches to light the way. Sit with her and listen for her guidance. Go to a crossroads or a doorway and feel the energy of making the decision. Allow the step you take to be the wisdom you need. *Irisanya*

February

February can be a month of change. Depending on where you are in the northern hemisphere, there can be days of thick snow, but also the first signs of spring. A common modern Pagan name for the Moon in February is Snow Moon, but another name is Budding Moon – and this can be when the first buds of flowers are seen poking through the soil.

Imbolc – the festival celebrating the start of the lambing season – and Valentine's Day both fall in February, so it is a month of new life and, perhaps, new romance.

In astrology, the Sun starts the month in Aquarius, the water carrier, which is the sign of the humanitarian. This is a good time of year to consider our place on the planet. It enters Pisces, the sign of the fishes, on or around February 19. This is associated with the God Neptune and the Goddess Venus. It represents mutability, change and transformation as well as emotional matters. Work magic to turn difficulties into opportunities and transform troubles with the power of love.

1. Imbolc: This major Celtic festival lies roughly halfway between the Winter Solstice and the Spring Equinox in the northern hemisphere. It is a turning point; a moment we may start to notice the days becoming longer, even though dark still outweighs light.

Get outside if you can. Look for that first snowdrop, the beginnings of a clump of crocuses or whatever greenery can be seen where you live. Feel the air on your skin; is it as cold as it was? Can you feel the promise of spring? Are birds singing when there was silence yesterday?

Brigid is the Lady of Imbolc; she is the Celtic Goddess of smithing, songs and poetry and much more, plus she is heavily associated with the return of spring. At dawn or dusk (liminal times) at Imbolc, light a candle to represent the returning light. Place a bowl by the candle with an oatcake in and some milk. Ask for Brigid's blessing and let her know this is her offering. Nothing more is required. Go about your day, be busy, be wise and be compassionate. Later on, discard the milk and the oatcake either in your garden (safely and hygienically!) or elsewhere away from your home. It will be eaten by creatures or simply return to the soil, reinforcing the cyclical nature of all things. *Mabh Savage*

2. Groundhog Day: This is an example of a Euro-Pagan holiday that was adapted to American soil. It probably originated in pre-Christian rites to the Bear Goddess, echoes of which survived in a folklore that the bear would wake from hibernation on the Christian holiday of Candlemas and predict the length of the remaining winter, based on her shadow. German settlers to Pennsylvania transferred this belief to the groundhog. According to Delaware Indian legends, the early animals went underground to escape the Great Flood. The groundhog was the first to re-emerge. For this reason it is regarded as a grandparent. Drum to summon the groundhog, then cheer and clap in appreciation. *Hearth Moon Rising*

3. Building a Relationship with Brigid: After Imbolc, continue to build a relationship with Brigid by creating an altar with her image. You might also include a flame for the forge, a bowl of water for the well and a feather for the aviary. Set a place for Brigid to come into your life. Spend time meditating with her regularly. Read about her and talk to her. Just like any relationship, you will want to keep showing up...and she will join you. *Irisanya*

4. Home Cleansing Ritual:

White 7-day container candle

Sage wand
One small quartz per room
Flat dish or tray

Place the candle in the center of the dish. Arrange the crystals and sage wand around the candle. Affirmation: *'May this candle of white fill this home with light.'* Repeat the affirmation as you light the candle. Focus and meditate on the purpose before removing the sage to smudge the home. Let the candle burn. Place one crystal per room. *Laeynarrie Auvresti.*

5. National Weatherperson's Day: This is observed in the USA and recognises individuals in the fields of meteorology, weather forecasting and broadcast meteorology, as well as volunteer storm spotters and observers. Research low-tech and traditional ways of predicting the weather that you could try out. You could fit a weathervane to your home. *Mélusine Draco*

6. Feast of St Dorothy, Patron of Gardeners and Flowers, and St Amand of Poitou, Patron of Winemakers, Brewers and Publicans: Many traditional English witches mark saints' days. Give a tribute to St Dorothy and St Amand in the form of food and wine – or have a go at planning a witch's garden to plant in the spring. *Mélusine Draco*

7. Favonius: This was the Roman festival of spring sowing. Scatter seed for the birds in homage, or plant early seeds indoors, in a greenhouse or a propagator. *Mélusine Draco*

8. Candle Spell for Springtime Wishes: You need a floating candle for each person present and a fireproof bowl or cauldron filled with water. Everyone should scratch their wish on the candle's bottom, light it and float it on the water. Chant three times:

Fire and water
Kindle and flow
Bring life to our dreams
And let them grow.

Afterwards, enjoy watching the candles burn down. **Lucya Starza**

9. O-tauesai: This rice-planting festival is a Japanese celebration of fertility. After the rice-planting ceremony, a ritual dance simulates a couple having sexual intercourse. Masked goblins also hand out ritual smacks with bamboo sticks to 'drive the devil out'. Research spring planting traditions and customs from the country in which you live. **Mélusine Draco**

10. An Apple Wish Spell: Take one apple and cut off the top. Using a teaspoon, hollow out the inside, making sure to retain the pips. Write your wish on some parchment and place it inside the apple with any of the following: apple pips and rose petals for love, cloves for luck, orange peel for health, an acorn for something to grow. Bury the apple in soil and let it work its magic. Do not return to see if it has grown, but have faith that it has. **Rebecca Beattie**

11. Festival of Ptah, God of Creativity: In ancient Egypt the first day of Rekehnedjes, which roughly equates to February, was the festival of Ptah, God of creativity and artisans. Prepare your craftworking space focusing on creative inspiration. Burn rosemary incense and light a yellow candle. Make offerings of food and scented oils. Recite: *'I am the clay, I am the wood, I am the song. Ptah, who shaped the world, guide my hands and my words, Anekh brak. All praise to you.'* **Carol Tierney**

12. Ariadne's Labyrinth: Take time to walk a labyrinth (a finger labyrinth will do) and allow Ariadne to guide you to those places deep inside you that need acknowledgment and healing. When you reach the center, take a few deep breaths and call to her:

Ariadne of the spiraling path,
Guide me to my own shadows.
Show me their value, their worth,
So I can understand their place in my life
And let them heal so I can grow.
Laura Perry

13. Imbolc, Oimelc, Lá Fhéile Bride, Calan Gaeaf (Old Style, Julian Calendar): Offer to a fire: dry herbs, whiskey, butter, ghee or incense. Invoke Brighid. Pour milk offerings on stones; honey, cider or milk in fields or gardens. Place a basket by the hearth or door with shortbread cookies, Brighid's crosses and blue stones. Wake the soil with a staff or stick. Sing or recite poetry to the trees. Offer a corn dolly to the Earth, burying it in the soil after saying a few words. This will grow to wheat for the following Lughnasad. *Ellen Evert Hopman*

14. Self Love Magick: While it might be Valentine's Day, remember that love transcends time and tradition. No matter if you're in a relationship or not right now, spend a few minutes with yourself. The first person who needs your love is you. Hold or stand by a mirror. Close your eyes, take a deep breath and then open your eyes. Looking at yourself deeply, say aloud: *'I love you.'* Repeat until you feel the love well up in your heart. *Irisanya*

15. Lupercalia: Lupercalia means festival of the wolves, part of weeklong Roman fertility rites. Ceremonies at this ancient festival were geared toward every stage of fertility: encouraging souls to seek birth, helping lovers come together, enhancing the fertility of young women and ensuring women already pregnant delivered safely. The Church turned this popular and persistent holiday into the tamer St Valentine's Day. Place a Valentine card on your altar for a few days to honor the loving nature of wolves and humans. *Hearth Moon Rising*

16. *'Adopt the Pace of Nature: Her Secret is Patience.'* **Ralph Waldo Emerson:** Go somewhere there are trees, look around, allow your gaze to rest upon a tree. Move slowly towards it, ask permission to place your hand on it and then feel the energy stored within. Turn and with your back against the tree, rest there knowing that like the tree you are filled with life force even when it feels as if nothing is happening. *Yvonne Ryves*

17. **Sheep Shearing and Blessings:** February is associated with spring; whispers of warmth to come as the new sheep are sheered and blessings of wool become available to devotees of spinning and weaving Goddesses. The shearing can be celebrated even by those who cannot participate in wool gathering. Place fiber tools on the altar along with images of a Goddess of spinning. Take this time to cleanse your tools and yourself with smudging and petition the divine for renewed inspiration in your work. *December Fields-Bryant*

18. **Start of Ash Tree Month in the Celtic Tree Calendar:** In winter, you can recognise ash trees without leaves because the twigs are upturned, the buds at the end of the shoots are black and the seeds grow in bunches, called keys. Keys hang in brown clusters in winter then fall to the ground in spring. In Celtic mythology, ash is the tree of life and touches the three worlds. Go outside and see if you can spot an ash tree; visualise it touching the three worlds of water (underground), land and sky. *Lucya Starza*

19. **Hachinohe Enburi:** This localised Japanese folk dance festival

dates back to when people with no experience of farming were taught how to work in the fields through dancing. This is a good opportunity for a children's introduction to growing things. *Mélusine Draco*

20. St Wulfric of Compton: He was also a seer with the gifts of prophecy and healing who became known as a healer of body, mind and spirit for all those who sought him out. Perform a small observation to request powers of healing and prophecy. *Mélusine Draco*

21. Feralia: This Roman religious holiday was sacred to Jupiter, in the guise of Jupiter Feretrius. The temples would be closed, then reopened at noon. This is an opportunity to take the day off in honour of the God. *Mélusine Draco*

22. Beating the Bounds: Traditional day for walking parish boundaries in England. The custom is thought to date back to Anglo-Saxon times and might even have been derived from the Roman festival of Terminalia, celebrated in honour of Terminus, God of landmarks. Cakes and wine were offered to him. Walk around your garden or the house you live in – or go further and walk around your town. Make an offering to Terminus and the spirits of your place. *Lucya Starza*

23. Grow Herbs: Most of us are suffering from the winter blues and are impatiently waiting for spring. To help with that, start an herb garden. Herbs can easily be cultivated in the home. Great ones to grow inside are basil, oregano, thyme, sage, rosemary and parsley. *Mycobacterium vaccae* in potting soil can trigger the brain to release serotonin. It is a natural way to relieve the winter blues. *Ravenwings*

24. Primrose Lore: Primroses are quintessential flowers of early spring in Europe. The name comes from the Latin *prima rosa*, meaning 'first rose'. They are associated with Freya, Norse Goddess of love, and are also a fairy flower. According to folklore, if they grow outside your house they will protect it and also attract fairies. Some tales suggest primroses give people the ability to see fairies, by eating their petals or placing a posy on a fairy mound. Add primrose petals to a spring salad. *Lucya Starza*

25. Feast of Montu: Make a request to the ancient Egyptian falcon-headed war God for the ending of all conflict in the world. *Mélusine Draco*

26. Big Hugs Candle Spell: You need a tealight, a jar and paper. From the paper, cut out a chain of paper dolls the right size to fit around the outside of the jar. Take the tealight out of its metal container and rub it between your hands, then put it back in the container before putting it in the jar with the dolls outside that. Light the candle and visualise yourself being hugged as it burns. You can reuse your chain of hugging dolls and jar; pop a new candle in when you want a magical hug. *Lucya Starza*

27. Equiria, Mars Gradius: This was celebrated in Ancient Rome with chariot races in honour of the God Mars and religious observances. The day had both a religious and military significance – rites were performed involving purification of the army. Pay tribute to those in the armed forces who are serving their country overseas or donate to a charity for injured soldiers. *Mélusine Draco*

28. Apple Wealth Cakes: Apple has long been the symbol of health, wealth, and happiness. Cinnamon, allspice, and nutmeg are also associated with wealth; putting them together often has amazing results! Timing is also important. Use this recipe spell on a morning at a new moon. Mix together:

1½ cups applesauce
1 cup sugar
½ cup oil
1½ cups flour
1 tsp salt
1 tsp baking soda
1 tsp cinnamon
½ tsp allspice
½ tsp nutmeg

Bake in greased muffin pans at 325 for 25 minutes. *Mary Burkett*

29. Leap Year Day: For the Gregorian calendar, an extra day was added in February every four years to balance out the seasonal cycles. To find more balance in yourself, cut out a fish shape to draw on the energy of this extra day in the astrological sign of Pisces. On one side write your positive qualities; on the reverse your negative qualities. Take the fish and drop into running water, declaring that as the fish swims you wish to become a more balanced person in life and love. *Rachel Mayatt*

March

While the Mediaeval name for the Moon in March is Chaste Moon and the Celtic name is Moon of Winds, another modern Pagan name for it is Death Moon. It serves as a reminder that death is a part of life and that many animals are struggling to find food if the weather is bad. March can be stormy and still cold. This is a good time to put out food for birds and other wildlife to help them survive.

In astrology the Sun moves from Pisces to Aries on or around March 21. The sign of the ram is the first in the Zodiac and is about new beginnings. A fire sign, it is associated with Mars, who is the Roman God of war, but also the guardian of growing crops. Call on this energy for spells of passion, action and adventure – for getting out and doing what you truly want as well as for championing good causes, particularly those associated with protecting the environment. However, Aries can cause impulsive behaviour, so think actions through before leaping in headfirst.

1. Crow Moon (Delaware Native American Name): Though our solar calendar is set, in nature the changing light of the Sun and Moon work together in yearly varying sequences to regulate the cycles of plants and animals. During the Moon that falls when the days and nights are balanced, the birds that stay through the winter become louder, more active, and more noticeable. Warm weather nesters have not yet arrived, but crows, ravens and other corvids announce the coming spring. Salute a corvid today. *Hearth Moon Rising*

2. Tea and Camellias: Camellias are among the brightest flowers to bloom in March in England. They bring colour to the greyest day. Camellias come from southern China. In 1725BC, the Chinese emperor discovered that an infusion of *camellia sinensis* leaves was his favourite drink. This became known as tea. Buddhist priests prized tea as a stimulant. They spread its popularity to Japan and developed the Japanese tea ceremony. Tea plants and ornamental camellias are closely related, but are not the same. Go for a walk and see what flowers are blooming, then enjoy a cup of tea and honour those in its history. *Lucya Starza*

3. Arachne's Day: Arachne, from Greco-Roman mythology, was a mortal and a talented weaver who challenged the Goddess Athena to a weaving contest. The versions of the story are many, and the outcome is both that she won and lost, but either way she gave her name to the insect classification of spiders. Weaving, from a magical viewpoint, can be both meditative and functional. Start weaving a tapestry of your life (entire or magical), incorporating different colours and textures of thread to represent different aspects. *Rebecca Bird*

4. Mad March Hares: The idea of hares going mad in March stems from their courtship rituals, in which they dance, box and leap. According to folklore, this behaviour linked hares to witches. It was thought this was also what witches got up to in covens. There are many folktales of witches shapeshifting into hares. In Roman mythology, the hare was a symbol of fertility and sex and was associated with the Goddess Venus. Next full Moon, look for the shape of the hare in it and make a wish. *Lucya Starza*

5. Serpent Mother's Wisdom: The Minoan snake Goddess is a major figure from ancient Crete. This time of year, snakes in Crete emerge from their burrows. Call on Serpent Mother to help you spring-clean your life physically and spiritually.

Oh Serpent Mother,

Whose wisdom penetrates the world,
Teach me to identify my own power
And wield it well,
And help me to discover the beauty
In letting go of things that no longer serve me.
Laura Perry

6. Kirishima Jingu Otaue-sai: A Japanese ceremonial rice-planting festival to mark the beginning of spring. Offer up a bowl of cooked rice in hope of a good 'harvest'. **Mélusine Draco**

7. March Storms and Blasting Rods: One English proverb says: *'If March comes in like a lion, it will go out like a lamb.'* Another saying goes:

When March blows its horn [thunder storms],
Your barn will be filled with hay and corn.

Neither of these weather predictions are scientifically accurate, but March weather can be stormy. Use the power of a March storm to magically charge a blasting rod – a staff used for clearing negative energy from any space. **Lucya Starza**

8. International Women's Day: A time to reflect on femaleness. Women may be half the world's population, but they are not yet standing as equals in authority, wealth or leadership. Today imagine the Goddess in everywoman showing her strength to the world. Reflect on the progress made, not the gaps and goals. Find your own female Self (men and women) and be unapologetic. Praise her hard work. Honor her perseverance. Celebrate her creativity. Then find a woman important to you and do the same for her. **Dorothy Abrams**

9. Best Foot Forward Walking Spell: I came up with this walking spell when I was regularly visiting someone in hospital and had little time to cast magic for healing. Visualise what you want as you walk, imagining each step bringing it closer and closer to you while you silently repeat these words to yourself in your head:

With each step I cast this spell
May all be right and all be well
Lucya Starza

10. St Kessog's Feast Day: Kessog was Scotland's patron saint before St Andrew, and his name was used as a battle cry by the Scots; soldiers had a special veneration for him. Son of the king of Cashel in Ireland, Kessog is said to have worked miracles, even as a child. Old Craft witches often called upon Christian saints to add strength to their spells, and those of Scottish lineage might find Kessog a useful ally since the Church often hijacked local heroes and turned them into saints – especially those able to perform miracles. *Mélusine Draco*

11. Johnny Appleseed Day: This celebrates the American pioneer nurseryman John Chapman who introduced apple trees to large parts of the USA and was nicknamed Johnny Appleseed. If you plant an apple seed, the tree that grows might bear apples that are different from the fruit of its parent. Eat an apple today in Johnny Appleseed's honour and research the history and folklore of the apple. *Mélusine Draco*

12. Aztec New Year: This is the celebration of the New Year according to the Aztec calendar and is generally considered to occur at sunrise on March 12. The holiday is still observed in some communities in Mexico, when ocote (pitch-pine) candles are lit on the eve of the New Year, along with fireworks, drumming and singing. *Mélusine Draco*

13. Protection from Bad Luck: Here is a traditional folk remedy if you are suffering from bad luck. Place onions or apples in the corner of each room to soak up negative energy. When the fruit or veg have gone black, take them far from your home and bury them. *Lucya Starza*

14. Ancient Egyptian Festival of Osiris, God of the Afterlife: Offer myrrh incense in remembrance of deceased family members. *Mélusine Draco*

15. Poem for the Day:

> *Medicine Man*
> *Healer and trickster,*
> *rattle and drum.*
>
> *Talks to spirits,*
> *on your behalf.*
>
> *Finds the herd,*
> *feeding the tribe.*
>
> *Dances for rain,*
> *refreshing Mother Earth.*
>
> *Old ways lost,*
> *when white-man came.*
> *Ronin Shaman*

16. Great Cosmic Mother-of-All and You: Explore the beauty of the cosmos. Spend some time looking up at the night sky or cruise the internet for images of the stars, the planets and the other wonders of space. Allow yourself to be in awe of this shifting, swirling, living universe that you're part of. If you feel so moved, offer up your thanks to Great Cosmic Mother-of-All for holding you in her vast and loving embrace. *Laura Perry*

17. Liberalia: The Roman festival of the God of wine, freedom and fertility, Liber Pater ('the free father'), and his consort Libera. The Romans celebrated Liberalia with processions, drinking, saucy songs and masks hung on trees. Have a go at making a ceremonial mask. This feast also celebrated boys maturing into manhood. If you have a teenage child, honour the fact that they are growing up. *Lucya Starza*

18. Hrethmonath: In *De Temporum Ratione*, Bede states that March was called Hrethmonath by the Anglo-Saxons because they made sacrifices to the Goddess Hretha then. Hretha means fame or honour, which suggests Hretha was a warrior like Mars, who gives us the modern name March. Hrethmonath marks the end of winter, so Hretha could be seen as the Goddess who battles and defeats winter. Mark the occasion by celebrating your own victories and deciding what fights are ahead for the coming year. **Carol Tierney**

19. Ostara Frittata:

1 onion
1 tbsp minced garlic
3 small tomatoes
1 pint mushrooms, quartered
8 cups spinach
2 blocks tofu, drained
1½ cup almond milk
½ cup nutritional yeast (cheese substitute)
¼ cup tamari
1½ tsp turmeric
½ tsp black salt

1 tbsp dill
1 tsp parsley flakes
1 tsp pepper

Sauté onion and garlic, add vegetables, sauté until wilted. Purée other ingredients in a food processor, pour over the top of the veggies in a baking pan. Bake at 375 for 30 minutes. *Amie Ravenson*

20. Apple Magic: The beautiful Norse maiden Goddess Idunn stands in the doorway to the light half of the year, offering the fruit of magic and immortality with which she nourishes the Asgardians. Devotion: Cut an apple in half, reflecting the dark and light halves of the year, chanting the prayer:

Blessed sparrow,
Who lights beauty in Nature.
Nourish me with simple things.

Eat the apple half designated as 'light' and place the other outdoors as an offering to Idunn. *Tiffany Lazic*

21. Guided Visualisation for the Spring Equinox: At the equinoxes, especially at the full Moon, the high and low tides are at their most extreme. Things long lost or hidden can be revealed. This meditation uses that imagery as a means of self-discovery or to answer a question. Sit comfortably in a safe place. Take three deep breaths, then close your eyes.

Imagine you are standing at the coast, above the beach, watching the sea. The tide is high. Picture the scene in your mind and watch it for a while. Think of a question. As the question forms itself in your mind, you notice the tide is going out. Watch as it recedes. More and more of the beach is revealed. What is it like? Is it rocky, sandy or pebbly?

Walk onto the revealed shoreline. The beach is wet, but safe underfoot. Follow the receding tide. Observe the shore at your feet as you go. The tide goes out further. You see something special has been uncovered. Go up to it. Study it. It can help you answer your question.

If there is something for you, take it. It is a treasure from the sea. When you are ready, return up the beach. When you have reached the top, open your eyes. *Lucya Starza*

22. Attis Arbour Intrat: In Ancient Rome, the procession of the pine trees was dedicated to Cybele, Ops or Rhea, in what was known as the Festival of the Entry of the Tree; also *Dies violae*, laying of flowers at tombs. Visit a grave or memorial of an ancestor of blood, place or tradition and leave flowers. *Mélusine Draco*

23. Tubilustrium: A day of special religious observance and sacred to Minerva, patroness of trumpets and also Roman Goddess of war and wisdom – you can make your choice. Have a go at playing a wind instrument in her honour. *Mélusine Draco*

24. Blessings of Birch Water: The Silver Lady of the Woods, sacred to the Goddess, Birch has many gifts, none so blessed as her life's blood. Birch water in spring is a sweet, detoxifying tonic full of micro-nutrients. This potion can be added to your spring rituals and spell work to aid in cleansing of the old and bringing in new patterns for life. As a living libation, birch water also makes a magical base for other intention setting and manifestation brews. *December Fields-Bryant*

25. The Cailleach: This day was known as Latha na Caillich, Cailleach Day or Lady Day. Right up to the 17th century in Scotland, March 25 was celebrated as the New Year and contests would be held to drive out the winter hag. Work with The

Cailleach to clear out any old or unwanted bad habits. She is associated with the rock and stone of the landscape so you could send any negative thoughts, issues and energy into a pebble then throw it away into the sea, running water or bury it in soil. **Rachel Patterson**

26. Rebirth: Spring is a time for rebirth, our own as well as the Earth's. For your transition into the coming year, wear an old scarf over your head, sit in the light of the Sun and say: *'Persephone, as you return the Earth is reborn.'* Shed the scarf, putting it to be recycled. Say: *'I too am reborn in your light, renewed like the coming year.'* Sprinkle some wildflower seeds in your garden as a mark of your rebirth this spring. **Jenny Cartledge**

27. Clear Energy: You need a rattle, drum or something that makes a noise. Hold the intention of clearing the energy within your home or workspace. Move slowly, taking your time, shaking the rattle or banging the drum. Be mindful of corners, bookcases, places where energy can get stuck. Your instrument may change tone or speed as it works, just allow it to play. Afterwards open all windows and doors to let the element of air in to complete the clearing. **Yvonne Ryves**

28. Yestarë: This is the Elven New Year – the first day of Tuilë, the Elven spring, and first of seven Elven feasts mentioned by Professor J. R. R. Tolkien in the Middle-Earth stories. In Tië eldaliéva, the Elven Path tradition, this meryalë (holiday) aligns with Vairë the Weaver. She resonates with the weaving of the threads of time: past, present, and future. Because of this, we can see her 'cutting' the fabric of the old year and beginning this year anew. **Calantirniel**

29. Egg Lore: Eggs are symbols of birth, resurrection and creation in cultures worldwide. In India, China, Ancient Egypt and

Ancient Greece, Gods, Goddesses – even life itself – were said to have hatched from eggs. In alchemy, the egg represents the four elements vital for life. The shell represents earth, the membrane represents air, the white represents water and the yolk represents fire. The crucible in which alchemists attempt to make the philosopher's stone is called the philosopher's egg. Meditate and visualise new life hatching. Consider what it means to you. *Lucya Starza*

30. Festival of Salus, Roman Goddess of Public Safety and Welfare: Her temple was on the Quirinal Hill. This is an appropriate time for magical intervention on health and safety issues. *Mélusine Draco*

31. Lunae in Aventino: Festival of Luna, Goddess of the Moon, who later became identified with Diana. Go outside tonight, observe the Moon and pour a libation in honour of the Goddess Luna. *Mélusine Draco*

April

In many lands in the northern hemisphere the woods and forests are becoming carpeted with spring flowers, while more flowers bloom in fields, hedgerows and gardens. Go outdoors and celebrate the springtime. Names for April's Moon include Growing Moon, Seed Moon and Pink Moon. When it is full, perform magic for growth, creativity and for your plans to blossom. Plant seeds to be watered by April showers and warmed by the increasing sunlight of the lengthening days.

In astrology, the Sun moves into the sign of Taurus the bull on or around April 21. Taurus represents strength, perseverance and virility, but also love, beauty and happiness in the aspect of Hathor, the great cow Goddess of Ancient Egypt. Try to keep this balance in your life. Taurus is also a practical Sun sign, so this is a good time to start practical projects.

Also, you can call on the power of the trickster Gods and Goddesses such as Loki or Eris to aid you with plans that require cunning, as April Fool's Day starts the month.

1. Poem for April Fools Day:

All Fools Day
Lord of Misrule, arise this day,
And come with us away to play.
King of Fools come play your tricks,
Let's see what stewpot you can mix
With upside-down and inside-out
To make us all bemused and doubt.
For only so will we begin
To reach for truth beneath the skin
Of reasoned folly, which is lies,
And for which we blind our eyes.

Open them with tricksy plays
That show the error of our ways.
Elen Sentier

2. International Children's Book Day, Hans Christian Andersen's Birthday: Try fairytale bibliomancy – pick a book of fairy tales, open it at random and read that story. What divinatory message does it have for you? *Lucya Starza*

3. Create a Mandala: Traditional mandalas were originally works of art containing symbols from Hindu and Buddhist spirituality, used for meditation. They were often circular. Create a modern, personal mandala. Get out paper, pencils, paints and pens. Draw a circle and fill it with symbols, shapes and patterns that are meaningful to you and colour it in, then meditate on it. *Lucya Starza*

4. Megalesia: Celebrate the ancient festival of Cybele, the Great Mother Goddess, who may have originated in Neolithic times. She was worshipped in Phrygia, Ancient Greece and Rome. Devotion: Outdoors, pour a libation to Cybele and say a prayer to the Great Mother Goddess.

Great Goddess, mountain-born Cybele
Ancient Deity of Motherhood and Mystery
My devotions I offer to you this day
In the acts that I do and the words that I say...
Lucya Starza

5. April Showers: It is easy to be gloomy when the weather takes a turn for the worst. It can ruin your day and change your plans, but here is a spell to see those silver linings within the rain clouds. Think of a project, write it down and plant it along with some grass seeds in a small pot. When those rains do come, take your pot outside and dance in the rain with it. See the silver raindrops nourishing your dreams... Now watch them grow! *Arietta Bryant*

6. Poem for the Day:

> *Rain drops.*
> *Wild flower petals.*
> *The earth is intensely focused on growing.*
> *Full of spring scents and green energy.*
> *Close your eyes.*
> *Take a deep breath.*
> *Move your awareness into your heart.*
> *Sense the liquid nature of that growing.*
> *Allow it to fill you up, to open you up.*
> *Ask, where am I growing?*
> *Where do I need to grow?*
> *Listen for the answer.*
> *Then blossom as only you can.*
> **Annette Wagner**

7. Spring Lessons: The year softens into spring as light returns. We are older, while the spring brings freshness and renewal. Contemplate the way that the line of our life meets the circles and cycles of the seasons. Each turn of the year brings new lessons and new reasons for gratitude. Light returns, and darkness will return, both having their place. Each in balance teaches us to be grateful for the other. *Nimue Brown*

8. Prayer for Clarity: *'Bless me with the clarity to see what is good in my life, to cherish the small beauties, the everyday wonders and the tiny gifts. Let me see the abundance in what I have, and how to better share that abundance so that I enrich this world as it enriches me. Knowing how I am blessed, may I find the courage to make needful changes that* *allow more goodness into my life.'* **Nimue Brown**

9. Poem for the Day:

Spring
Colour returns,
flowers and blossom.
Smells to entice
and wonder.

Magpie swoops,
protecting babies;
nest-ridden squawking.

Backyard,
bursts with life.
Barbie reignites.

Hay-fever,
is a bitch.
Ronin Shaman

10. Holy Mother Earth: Take time to connect to the Earth. Find a patch of ground (dig through snow if you have to) and crumble the dirt between your fingers. Breathe in its scent. The soil is a living thing, full of microbes and tiny organisms that are just as alive as you are. The soil grounds us. Our lives extend upwards from it. Greet Mother Earth and take a moment to offer her your gratitude. *Laura Perry*

11. Poem for the Day:

The Psychic Ones
Be aware

Of the psychic ones
The ones whose giggles light up the room
As well as your heart
Be aware
Of the sensitive ones
The ones who cry for what you think is no reason
As well as those who have every reason
Be aware
Of the little ones
The ones who can turn your life upside down
As well as be the reason you smile so much.
Ronikka Hubert

12. International Day of Human Space Flight: On this day in 1961, Soviet cosmonaut Yuri Gagarin became the first human to travel into outer space and perform the first manned orbital flight. In 1981, the first Space Shuttle, Columbia, was launched. If the sky is clear tonight, stargaze and meditate on how much we can all achieve if we try. *Lucya Starza*

13. Grounding Meditation: Get in a relaxed meditative state, then begin to focus on your center (usually the root or sacral centers). From this spot, push your energy down in a root-like fashion, using the imagery of a tree root digging deep into the ground. After your roots are placed, visualize negativity within you as a black fog and begin to collect and push the fog out of your root system. Once cleared, reverse the energy flow to bring Earth energy into yourself. *Laeynarrie Auvresti*

14: Poem for the Day:

Journey
Touch the land, feel the beat of the Earth.
Walk in the rain, feel the giver of life.

Open your arms to the wind, feel the power of nature.
Turn your face to the Sun, feel the heat of our crucible.
Walk the path that opens before you.
Ronin Shaman

15. Rusalja: The holiday for the Rusalki (river spirits) among the Lemko people of Carpathia. Other Slavic cultures have their Rusalki holiday on different days depending on local agricultural cycles. Ritual: Young women put on white dresses and join hands in a circle. Dance sunwise one complete turn. Then chant: *'The river is running, the season is turning, we Rusalki bless the land.'* Raise hands in blessing toward the land. **Erin Lale**

16. Spring Clean: Tidy the house, re-arrange cluttered cupboards or tend to an overgrown garden. Don't forget about yourself too – it's important to cleanse your spiritual aura. Smudging your body with sage, by wafting the smoke from the burning herb, is a powerful way to shake off negative energy and build up psychic protection. If you live in an area that's frequented with April showers, collect this energetic water to purify your crystals or gemstones. **Mark Anthony Terry**

17. Money Spell: In a Sunday Jupiter hour, when the new Moon is in Taurus, light three green candles in a triangle. Burn patchouli incense. Drink mint tea after each of nine repetitions of this charm to Lakshmi:

Of all thing hidden and all things seen
We could use a lot more green,
Smackers, dollars, semolians and bucks
Through prayer, hard work and a little luck
We ask for nothing we don't deserve
Just a stream of cash with a little reserve
Rev. Su Windsong

18. Make Faerie Rocks: Work magick that is great to do with kids and make faerie rocks for your garden. Simply get some smooth river or seaside rocks and clean them. Paint them with glitter paint or sprinkle glitter over the wet paint. You can use permanent markers to add words or images and then, when they are dry, seal them with a polyurethane type of sealer. Place them in your garden for the Fae! *Ravenwings*

19. St. Expeditus: Need help in a hurry? A speedy resolution? Or maybe you're a repentant procrastinator? Good news! There's an (unofficial) saint for that: St. Expeditus. Although Wired magazine calls this Armenian martyr 'patron saint of nerds', he's venerated by Latin American Catholics, hoodoo practitioners and Santerians (although Church hierarchy distances itself from him). His icon depicts him stomping on a crow that has a ribbon in its mouth with the word cras – Latin for 'tomorrow'. Sometimes he holds a clock; others, a cross with the word hodie (today). *Janet Boyer*

20. Prayer to Blodeuedd:

> *Blodeuedd, lady of the flowers,*
> *Wildness walking the world,*
> *Reaching for the Sun that turns and turns again.*
> *Blodeuwedd, silent soaring owl,*
> *Guide us to our true selves,*
> *Gliding through the night that turns and turns again.*

(Pronunciation: Blodeuedd = Blod-eye-eth, Blodeuwedd = Blod-eye-weth.) *Halo Quin*

21. Visit your Favourite Tree: Check in with it. Is it blossoming? Sleeping? Ask it to tell you something important. At home, research something about the tree's biology, history or lore. *Halo Quin*

22. Earth Day: On Earth Day, around the world, everyone is encouraged to switch off their lights from 8pm-9pm to raise awareness of our relationship to energy usage and the Earth's resources. Honour the Earth and the nourishing darkness of the soil, night and dreams. Ritual: Switch off all electrical appliances in your home. Create sacred space in your usual way. Feel the ground beneath you. Spend time contemplating the peace and darkness. Imagine you are a seed in the darkness, how does it feel? Slowly allow your seed-self to sprout in the darkness and grow into a plant, rooted in the Earth. What do you grow into? What can you, as a being of the Earth, offer back to Mother Earth? Light a candle and ponder the light held in the darkness. Make a pledge to honour the Earth. Close up, make notes and come back to everyday awareness. *Halo Quin*

23. Shakespeare Day: Some historians claim April 23rd for William Shakespeare's birthday, so what better day to celebrate the joy of words? Have a go at your own word play by making an acrostic with your name. Mine could be:

Mischievous
And
Beyond
Hope

You can use this technique to work some additional gusto into spells, for example:

Hear my words
Ease her pain
Aid my friend
Let sickness wane.

This chant, to aid in healing magic, has emphasis lent by the word 'heal' being built by the lines of the verse. Play around and find what works for you. *Mabh Savage*

24. International Sculpture Day: This is a day of appreciating sculpture in communities across the globe. Visit a gallery, museum or other public space with statues from our ancient Pagan past – or have a go at creating your own sculpture. You could use air-drying clay to make a Goddess or God figurine for your home or altar. *Lucya Starza*

25. Robigalia: This was a Roman festival where sacrifices were made to protect grain fields from disease. The celebration included chariot races, games and a blood sacrifice. The prayer is quoted in Ovid's *Fasti*, Book IV. It begins: '*Scaly Mildew, spare the blades of corn, and let their tender tips quiver above the soil. Let the crops grow, nurtured by favourable stars, until they're ready for the sickle.*' Modern celebrations can use organic plant food as the offering. This would be a great day to start composting. *Carol Tierney*

26. New Moon Magick: Here's a simple way to call something new into your life. Take a candle and hold it in your hand. Think about what you want, picture it clearly and allow that energy to move from you into the candle. Use a pin or a pen to carve into the candle a word or phrase to solidify your intent, if you like. Burn the candle fully on this night or light it a few minutes each evening. *Irisanya*

27. Beltane Quinoa Salad:

   2 cups quinoa, prepared per directions
   2 cups fresh asparagus, cut into 2 inch lengths, steamed until tender crisp
   1 cup sliced black olives

½ cup roasted red peppers, chopped
¼ cup fresh basil

Dressing
⅓ cup balsamic vinegar
½ cup olive oil
¼ cup lemon juice
1 tbsp garlic minced
1 tsp dried parsley
1½ tsp agave nectar
½ tsp salt
½ tsp pepper

Combine ingredients, add dressing. Allow to marinate for an hour or more. *Amie Ravenson*

28. Start of Floralia: Five-day festival of Flora, Goddess of flowers and springtime, celebrated in Ancient Rome. Traditional weather lore: *'Sweet April showers/Do spring May flowers.'* (From a poem written in 1610) Meditation: Plant or pick a flower and meditate on it each day for five days. *Lucya Starza*

29. Poem for Taliesin's Birthday:

Gwion bach, little one, stirring patiently,
Hare and salmon, wren and seed, flee from Cerridwen!
She your mother, she your fear, she your guardian,
Set afloat across the sea, reborn Taliesin!

Inspire now our work and play and creativity,
Shining bright and singing clear our blessed sacred song.
Guide us as we make our way through all our many forms,
Let us be now what we are and know our way 'ere long!
Halo Quin

30. May Eve: A truly magical time. Look out for fairies! And not the twinkly kind... If the hawthorns are flowering near you, collect some May blossom, ideally before or at dawn, and hang it over your door. This will help protect you from the more mischievous of the Fae. If the blossom is yet to come, some hawthorn or rowan leaves will have the same effect. Ask the tree's permission, always say thank you and leave an offering if possible. *Mabh Savage*

May

May starts with the Pagan fertility festival of Beltane, so celebrate all the joys of life and love. Spring has well and truly sprung and 'Summer is Icumen In', as the song goes. All around is greenery and blossom; birds are nesting, bees are buzzing and flowers are blooming. In the northern hemisphere all of this month can feel like a time to party. Be passionate; dance, sing or bang a drum; get creative.

The name of the May's Moon is Flower Moon. Go outside and connect with the land, greet the Sun and learn about the folklore and customs of your area. While Taurus the bull rules the start of the month, in astrology the Sun moves into Gemini on or around May 21. The sign of the twins is all about versatility. Let your creativity turn to things like writing or other forms of communication.

1. Beltane: This festival is celebrated about halfway between the Spring Equinox and Summer Solstice, which in the northern hemisphere falls around May 1. An agricultural holiday, some scholars believe Beltane started with the Egyptians, Greeks and Romans as May Day, and later evolved as the Celtic holiday Beltane and the Germanic festival of Walpurgis.

The earliest celebrations of Beltane often included sexual rites and large bonfires. One might leap over a smaller fire to bless themselves and a partner for the next year. In addition, celebrants would often make sacrifices to encourage prosperity of the land and livestock. On this holiday of fertility and growth, some celebrate by dancing around a Maypole, twirling colored ribbons in a simple dance. Rituals often focus on the return of the Sun as many once believed the Sun was held prisoner until it was released in the spring.

No matter what you choose to do this Beltane, think of the

things you want to birth into your life – ideas, actions and maybe a human being. This is a time to dance all of your desires into existence. *Irisanya*

2. Listen to your Heart: Reach down and touch the Earth. Feel it touch you back. Breathe in the energy of spring, full of May Day blessings. Close your eyes. Ask your heart, what do you desire today? Listen for the answer. Allow a word or two to emerge. Write it down, draw a symbol. Set an intention to listen to your heart every day. Then, walk your path filled with your heart's desire. *Annette Wagner*

3. A Bubbly Spell for Happiness: Go outside with bubble mixture on a sunny day. Picture in your mind something that fills you with joy and delight. Imagine sending those happy thoughts into bubbles as you blow them. Do this with as many joyful images you can think of. As each bubble bursts, happiness is released into the world, where it will grow. In the future, you will find a bubble of happiness returned to you in your own life. *Lucya Starza*

4. May the 4th Be With You!: The Jedi Church is a modern nontheistic religion that believes there is one all-powerful force that binds all things in the universe together. The Jedi Church believes that morality is an innate sense. Today is a good day to quiet your mind and contemplate the duality of light v dark. Listen to the force within you. Emotion, yet peace. Ignorance, yet knowledge. Passion, yet serenity. Chaos, yet harmony. Death, yet the Force. *Carol Tierney*

5. Blessing of the Ships: In ancient Crete, the heliacal rising of the Pleiades in the late spring heralded the beginning of the Minoan sailing season. This is the time to call on Grandmother Ocean to bless your travels, whatever your vehicle may be:

Posidaeja, whose waters embrace the world,
Please embrace me as I travel.
Bless my comings and goings
Both near and far,
So I may discover wonders and joy
And return home safely
At my journey's end.
Laura Perry

6. Connect with the Land: Take a few minutes to put your feet or hands on the Earth and truly feel your connection with the land beneath you. If you can, then walk for a while and let the shape of the Earth act on your body. Contemplate your connection with the land you live on, the people who were there before you and those who will come after. Meditate on your own place in the history and future of your land. *Nimue Brown*

7. Academic Anxiety Relief Spell: In a Wednesday Moon hour, with the Moon in Virgo, burn a pentacle of candles: silver, purple, white, blue and orange. Drink some chamomile tea and place in a bag with a honeycomb sigil some skullcap, anise and a dried bean after each of five repetitions of this charm to Athena and Odin:

Organized and yet relaxed
My mind shall not be overtaxed
Joy in knowledge is true power
Change my mind within the hour
Rev. Su Windsong

8. Poem for the Day:

Forest
Dappled light shining

through the leaves.
Deep in The Green
walking with trees.

Dark and dangerous
or light and friendly.
Home for the hunter;
hide-out for the rascal.

Lungs of Gaia,
given emphysema,
by the stupidity
of human 'progress'.

A breath of fresh air,
fills you
with the promise
of life.

Followers of the Old Ways
can be seen,
deep in The Green
talking with trees.
Ronin Shaman

9. Child Bedtime Protection Spell: Instruct the child to form a circle with their hand, using the thumb and forefinger. This circle is placed near their mouth. As they imagine being comfortable and safe in bed, they should to recite the spell and then blow through the circle, as if blowing a bubble. Have them aim at the bed and visualize a protective bubble surrounding it. Recitation: *'Blow a bubble around my bed, so I may safely lay my head.'*
Laeynarrie Auvresti

10. An Incense to Bring Love:

1 tbsp damar pearls
½ tbsp myrrh
A sprig of forget-me-not flowers
½ tbsp of rose petals
10 drops of rose essential oil

Begin by grinding the dried flowers in a pestle and mortar, then add the resin and finally the essential oils. Fill a censer with salt or sand, then place a lit charcoal disc on top. Sprinkle on the incense, making sure you keep the windows open and the room well aired. *Rebecca Beattie*

11. Greet the Sun: Start your morning with a greeting to the Sun. Stand outside in the sunlight or by a window. Raise your arms and say:

Greetings, oh Sun,
You who are known by many names,
Apollo, Dagr, Helios, Ra,
I give thanks for your blessings of light and warmth,
For your energy and all the life you sustain.
I bid you hail and welcome.

You may write your own greeting or speak straight from your heart. *Jenny Cartledge*

12. Old Beltane, May Day, Lá Bealtaine, Calen Mai (from the Julian Calendar): Offerings to fire: Dry herbs and flowers, whiskey, butter, ghee, incense. Invoke The Daghda. Offer butter, milk, May wine or mead to stones and in fields or gardens. Make offerings of apples, berries, blossoms, rose flowers, savory, May wine, milk or honey to water, trees and land spirits. Dance around a fire, May bush or Maypole, wearing a crown of flowers. *Ellen Evert Hopman*

13. Wishing Tree: May brings the promise of the summer to come. Celebrate the changing season with some resolutions. Take strips of biodegradable coloured ribbon or paper; write a wish, a promise or even a blessing on each piece; walk barefoot into the garden and tie them onto a bush or tree. Increase the magickal energy by adding wind chimes, sparkly streamers and suncatchers as well, if you have permission to leave non-biodegradable items. *Arietta Bryant*

14. Return to All-Day-Life: After the ceremonies and the festivals of Beltane (and Samhuinn), this day brings a turning back to all-day-life. People are a bit introverted, the memories are still vivid, but sadly quickly fading. Take stock of where you stand; in your family life, in your studies, in your work. Being under the sign of Taurus and after all the energy-consuming activities, have a copious meal. There is every reason for it! *Hennie van Geel*

15. Declutter: Go through your stuff. Look at what you have surrounded yourself with. Do all these things still function and, if so, do they still have a purpose in your life? If not, why not get rid of them? Look for people, second-hand shops and charity hand-outs where your things will still be of use. Don't hesitate, share what no longer serves you, but what might help other people. Be no longer weighed down by the unnecessary. *Hennie van Geel*

16. Say Goodbye to Bad Relationships: Following yesterday's clean-up, look at your relationships. Nobody has to stay in a bad relationship; this includes your ties with neighbours, friends and family. Is there anyone you should perhaps say goodbye to? Must you really take part in all those family gatherings? Can you loosen ties? For many people it is hard to take these kind of actions, but must you suffer under the attentions of anyone you don't actually like? *Hennie van Geel*

17. Let Your Star Shine: After cleaning up, it's time to let your star shine. Magic is all around, or more precisely, the initial stages of magical work are abounding. Remember the days of magic, when all the world shone with the light of expectation. Go out if you can and look for the odd things out, which could perhaps be used in works of true magical action. Don't hesitate, perform your magic! *Hennie van Geel*

18. Birth of the Greek Gods Artemis and Apollo: These twins are the children of Zeus and Leto. Artemis was the guardian of young women and Apollo the guardian of young men. Both Artemis and Apollo were skilled archers and hunters. Artemis was gifted a silver bow by her father, which had been made by the Cyclopes, while at Troy Apollo devastated the Greek Army with his arrows. Try your hand at archery, or head into the woods and sit as a hunter would, awaiting prey. See what speaks to you from the forest. *Jo Robson*

19. Neith: From Greco-Egyptian mythology, Neith was a Goddess of weaving and part of her hieroglyph resembled a loom. Cord-making, or braiding, is a form of weaving on a lucet, believed to date back to the Viking or Mediaeval periods. Lucet cord is square, strong, does not unravel if cut, and is a suitable method of making very long cords. Traditionally it would have been used on clothing, or to hang items on belts, but you could make your own to do knot spellwork. *Rebecca Bird*

20. Buddha's Birthday, or Vesak: This is celebrated at the time of the full Moon in May. Anyone, anywhere, of any spiritual path can follow the Buddhist principles of being kind and compassionate to fellow humans on this day. *Lucya Starza*

21. Nost-na-Lothion: An Elven feast, Nost-na-Lothion is the birth of flowers festival. Tolkien's stories mark this as beginning Elven summer, Lairë. The Elven Path aligns the feast with golden-haired Vána the Ever-Young. She has dominion over new green plant growth and flowers, and invites you to plant your seeds of intention to grow among the flowers. Once your seeds are planted, your heart is uplifted and you might see the Elves of Gondolin, the Elven City, begin to dance! *Calantirniel*

22. Feast of Elen Luyddog, of the Ways, of Old Tracks and Wells: Light a candle. Visualise a track through a forest and begin to walk. What life obstacles are there? Ask for inspiration on how to remove them. As you walk, see the gifts in your life, and project your desires ahead. At the end of the track is a spring. Drink deep, and ask: *'Elen, show me the way to achieve my dreams.'* *Caroline Wise*

23. Poem for the Day:

> *River*
> *White and racing,*
> *or clear and calm.*
> *Water soothing me*
> *with gurgling song.*
>
> *Net and spear,*
> *or hook and line.*
> *Water feeding me,*
> *with gurgling song.*
>
> *In life and death,*
> *body and soul.*

Water guiding me
with gurgling song.
Ronin Shaman

24. Standing in Sovereignty: In Canada, as Victoria Day is celebrated, the name of ancient Brigantia echoes softly in the festivities. Sovereign queen, life-supporting land, and protector, 'The Exalted One' gave her name to the Celtic tribe the Brigantes, exercising wisdom and discernment. Devotion: Stand tall, imagining a spear in one hand and a globe in the other, chant: *'Exalted Brigantia, guide my eyes to see clearly, my feet to step surely, and my heart to remain strong and true.'* **Tiffany Lazic**

25. Halley's Comet: A passage of Halley's Comet was observed on this day in 240BC by scholars in China, where it was believed to be a broom star, clearing evil from the heavens. Use that image as basis of a visualisation to see all that harms the Earth being swept away. **Lucya Starza**

26. A Prayer to Frigga to Bless a Child:

All-Mother of the hearth
Wrap my child in your protection.
Solicitor of oaths, Minder of mistletoe
Let nothing harm my child.
Beloved of Aesir, Mother of Golden Baldr
Secure my child from those that do ill
Lady of Fensalir enthroned on Hliðskjál
Shelter my child when they are far from home
Daughter of Fjorgynn
May my child's footsteps lead to safe-keeping
Lady of the Spindle
Guide my child's hands from misdeeds
Far-seeing Seer

Let me see where my child wanders
December Fields-Bryant

27. Stretch Yourself Creatively: Take some time to really look at what's around you, then try to capture that on paper. A pen and the back of an envelope will do. Go for colour if you can. Put down shapes and lines; don't worry about how anyone might judge you, just allow the day to flow through you and onto the page. It's good to let loose and play a little, so give yourself permission to do that. If you aren't visual, get some clay you can shape with instead. **Nimue Brown**

28. Seasons Meditation: Sit in a quiet place, take a few deep breaths and contemplate each visualisation in turn:

Summer
The warm scent of flowers;
Distant music.

Autumn
Dead leaves dance in the wind.
And tug at you to join them.

Winter
A storm howls in darkness.
You hear its hunger.

Spring
Clouds scud across the sky.
Early birds fly back to nest.
Lucya Starza

29. Oak Apple Day: This was once a public holiday in England to commemorate the restoration of the monarchy in May 1660.

Festivities are still held on this day in some areas, in which a man dressed in garlands of flowers leads a parade. This may be associated with older Pagan celebrations of nature. Learn about traditional folk customs in your area at this time of year. *Lucya Starza*

30. Joan of Arc: About the age of 12, French peasant Joan of Arc had visions from saints Michael, Catherine and Margaret. They implored her to drive the English from French territory. Joan then successfully predicted a military reversal at the Battle of Rouvray, near Orléans. Charles VII and others believed her revelations to be divinely inspired after vetting and testing. Victorious campaigns followed, some resulting in crossbow wounds. She was eventually captured and ransomed; the English bought her for 10,000 gold coins and burned her at the stake, not so much for unproven heresy, but for cross-dressing (she wore her military clothes to prevent molestation). *Janet Boyer*

31. International No Tobacco Day: This day is a good day to look at any kind of addiction, regardless of what it is. Have a black ribbon or wool and an object representing addiction – a cigarette, picture of a glass of wine, chocolate, etc. Wrap the item with the black ribbon/wool slowly, repeating: *'Bind this desire, burn away with fire.'* Burn the wrapped object in a metal cauldron afterwards and scatter the ashes in the garden. *Rachel Mayatt*

June

In astrology, the Sun moves into Cancer at the time of the northern hemisphere's Summer Solstice, around June 21. Cancerians are people of great empathy. The powers of the sign of the crab can be tapped into at this time of year for magic to do with water, the emotions, intuition and to boost your own empathic abilities. However, also take care to protect yourself emotionally and magically because of the high emotional states associated with Cancer.

One of the names for this month's Moon is Rose Moon and roses are the flowers most associated with feelings and sentiments. Other Pagan names for the Moon in June are Strawberry Moon and Mead Moon – perfect food and drink to share at a midsummer night's ritual.

1. Festival of Cardea, Roman Goddess of Hinges and Doors: Light a candle; hail Cardea. Steep hawthorn leaves in boiling water, let cool. Remove debris and dust from hinges of significant doors. Oil if necessary. Wash the doors. Ask Cardea to protect your boundaries. Open your doors for cleansing air to blow through. Hang small branches of hawthorn on doors. Give thanks to Cardea and blow out the candle. *Caroline Wise*

2. The Melissae: These Minoan bee Goddesses from ancient Crete connect us with the sweet things in life. Light a beeswax candle and pour a libation of milk and honey to honor them. If you listen closely, they can tell you how to find joy in whatever life may bring.

Buzz around me,
Sweet Melissae,
And help me taste

The honeyed sweetness of life.
Laura Perry

3. Space Clearing: The sound of a bell is meant to carry on far, far away from anything our human ears can detect and so they are wonderful for space clearing. If you don't have a bell, an empty wine glass will do. It is the sudden sound that shakes the energy up, so experiment and find what suits you. Two coins being clashed together? Rapping on a table top? Rattling the dog's lead? Shaking your bangles? Take the coins out of your purse and put them in a little bag for this. Open the window to let the negativity out. Go to the centre of the room first and then the four corners. You will hear different sounds so give special attention to the dull areas. *Geraldine Beskin*

4. St Saturnia: The Catholic Church celebrates St Saturnia today as she is recognised as a virgin martyr. Why today's ladies might like to acknowledge her is because she is the patron saint of wine merchants! Fashions change and we drink so much wine nowadays but, when we slow down and actually do a little ritual, we sip our wine. We dedicate it to whichever aspect of the Goddess in her Many Guises we are working with and it tastes so sweet and 'different' then. St Saturnia also protects farmers, so spare a thought for the ideal weather conditions they will need to have a good harvest. *Geraldine Beskin*

5. Go for a Walk: The beginning of June can be windy, but as the days are long, it doesn't matter much. These bright, chilly days are times to go for a brisk walk around the park, plotting what you want to get done over the summer. Leave tense teenagers behind and find space in your head for what to do when their exams are done and before the dreaded results arrive. Use the crisp wind to blow away cobwebs and 'use' the movement in the grass, leaves and your hair to refresh yourself. *Geraldine Beskin*

6. Birthday of Alex Sanders, King of the Witches: He was a real Gemini. Cheeky, amazingly quick-witted, fast of speech, charismatic and sometimes unreliable. He appeared in the newspapers every week it seemed as his coven were 'sky clad' – or naked to you and I. He was a good leader, a good teacher and, if he hadn't been so public about witchcraft, perhaps it would have faded quietly way again. His popularity enabled a lot of books to be published and who can imagine life without crystals and candles now? *Geraldine Beskin*

7. Flowers: June's flowers are connected with new beginnings. Lavender is all around and has so many good aspects. Youth is about being supple and finding life fun, so use lavender to loosen joints. It is a great comforter and good to sweeten baths to get rid of exhaustion. Then scent your bedding with it for a calming, healing sleep as it soothes nerves too. Mercury, God of communication, and Iris, Lady of the Rainbow that bridges Earth and Sky, are messengers like Geminis. Purple, pink or especially yellow, are all good for good news. *Geraldine Beskin*

8. World Oceans Day – Oceans of the World Ritual: Collect water in a glass bowl, seawater if possible, rain water if not. Stir the water anti-clockwise saying: *'May all plastics and poisons be gone from the oceans.'* Then stir it clockwise saying: *'May the oceans be healed and whole.'* Charge with clear, bright light and picture healthy seas full of life. Return the water to the sea (directly or via a river) to carry the healing around the world. You could also volunteer for a beach-cleaning day. *Halo Quin*

9. Full Moon Magick: Stand under the light of the full Moon (or where the light would be if the sky was clear). Allow the light to touch your skin and take in all of the blessings. Remind yourself of all the beautiful things you've brought into your life since the previous full Moon and give thanks to the stars. Place any jewelry or magickal items you want blessed in the moonlight. Wear them this month and recharge them in the next month's moonlight. *Irisanya*

10. A Prayer of Self-Dedication: *'Lord and Lady of all that is, you who help the Earth spin and the Moon to hold her course, bless the body of your priest(ess) and guide me as I walk your ways. May I recognise those in need, and bring comfort where I can. Help me to approach each moment with fresh eyes and an open heart, help me to see the magic in everything. May I continue to walk your path with gladness, and hear your call and answer with grace.'* **Rebecca Beattie**

11. Make a Wand: Go for a walk in woods – or a park or garden – and find a fallen stick to make a wand. Find one that feels right to you, but do not cut one from a living tree without permission. Ask the spirits of the place for their blessings. Try to identify the tree it came from and say thank you. Take your wand home, trim and sand the rough edges. You can decorate it further if you want. *Lucya Starza*

12. Poem for the Day:

The Tree
Soldier of the forest
Standing guard
Home to many
And shield to many more.
Slow and eternal
Patient and loyal
No fair-weather friend,
You give unconditionally.
Deep roots, thick skin,
Shady branches, reaching wide
Sweet sap running

Magickal and majestic,
Timeless,
Tree.
Arietta Bryant

13. Birthday of Gerald Brosseau Gardner (1884–1964): Gerald Gardner is known as the Father of Wicca and was hugely influential in the history of modern Pagan witchcraft. He founded the Bricket Wood coven, wrote several books on magic and witchcraft, and helped Gardnerian Wicca spread worldwide. He did this after his retirement, proving that you are never too old to take up a new cause. What might you do? *Lucya Starza*

14. Birthday of the Muses – Spell to Call Your Muse: You will need a blue candle and a piece of paper. Write on the paper what you need inspiration with and set it on your altar or table. Light the blue candle in the morning. Say:

Clio, Euterpe, Thalia, Melpomeni, Terpsichore, Erato, Polymnia,
Ourania and Calliope gather round.
By air and fire
Flame burning higher
Hear my desire and inspire me.
Let the candle burn out. **Morgana Phenix**

15. Daisy Spell for Overcoming Indecision: If you are in a dilemma, pick a daisy and say: *'Daisy, daisy, give me your answer, do. I'm half crazy not knowing what to choose.'* Pull each petal off, asking, *'Should I do this?'* as you pluck one petal, then, *'Should I do that?'* as you pluck the next. Visualise each option. In the traditional daisy game, whatever the last petal represents is the correct answer, but for this spell you will know your correct answer by how you feel about it. *Lucya Starza*

16. A Prayer to Frigga for Brides and Wives:

Queen of Asgard, faithful wife of the All-Father
Keeper of the keys to the hall
Lead me to walk in your footsteps
Guide my steps on the path of the wife.
She who keeps Odin's secrets
Silent seer of the spindle
Help me to keep my own counsel
Let not my tongue wander nor cut my beloved.
Lady of the Langobards, wearer of the golden necklace
Let me take on only what enhances
and not lose myself in my love.
December Fields-Bryant

17. Joyful Cauldrons for Family, Friends, or the Whole Coven:
Give each person a jar with holes in the lid. Decorate your jars with lots of sparkle and write 'happiness', 'joy', 'harmony', or other words of intent on the jar to make it your 'Joyful Cauldron'. Light candles outside at sunset and, if you are in an area that has them, watch lightning bugs emerge! Catch them in your jars and ask them to bless you, sing them a spellsong if you like. Then release them and share some lemonade. *Mary Burkett*

18. Solstice Water: Summer Solstice is an excellent time of year for water. Rivers and lakes look so inviting sparkling in the sun and are so refreshing to body and soul. Collect some water from a place that is especially refreshing to you. Keep it in a beautiful closed container (or tabletop fountain) and bless it on your altar if you like. Use it in rituals and spellwork throughout the year, placing the container or fountain at the water station of your circle. *Mary Burkett*

19. Litha Veggie Skewers:

2 zucchinis (courgettes)
2 summer squashes
Pint cherry tomatoes
1 sweet onion
8 medium portabello mushrooms
1 red pepper

Sauce
⅔ cup soy sauce
2 tsp minced garlic
2 cups brown sugar
2 tsp ginger powder
½ cup lemon juice

Cut veggies into bite-size pieces and arrange on skewers. Drizzle with sauce, coating evenly. Bake at 375 for 30 minutes, turning once. Serve over rice drizzled with sauce from the pan. Garnish with chopped green onions. *Amie Ravenson*

20. Watching the Ferns: Traditional folklore says that if you watch the ferns on Midsummer Eve and collect the seeds that fall at exactly midnight, you can use them to render yourself invisible. Actually, ferns don't produce seeds – they have spores – but maybe spores have the same effect. Other folk tales say that if you sit among ferns at midnight on the Solstice Eve you will see fairies who might lead you to treasure. *Lucya Starza*

21. Midsummer Solstice:

Antlered one, your day is come,
Hold the light of summer Sun.
Fire the Goddess to the heart,

So your seed shall play its part
Down in the darkness that will come,
In winter season of the womb.
Oak King of summer, flower now
Hang garlands bright about your brow
To give us joy, the Lady too,
For she knows us as she knows you,
And with your seed she makes us new.
We light the fires and leaping through
We honour you.

The Oak King is one form of Gwyn ap Nudd, the antlered one who partners our antlered reindeer Goddess, Elen of the Ways. He holds the Midsummer Solstice – the three-day standstill of the sun, where the Sun appears to rise at the same place on the horizon for three days. The Sun moves on again on 24th June. This is the highpoint of the Sun's arc, from now until Midwinter there is less and less light each day, until the turnaround at the Midwinter Solstice, which we call Sun-Return. The Oak King's seed sparks the Goddess and goes down into her womb to be reborn next spring. Honour this, the longest day, with fire and feasting, and songs and dancing. ***Elen Sentier***

22. Skirophoria: This was a fertility festival in Ancient Greece. Priests and priestesses from the cults of Athena, Poseidon and Helios would lead a procession to the Skiron, a place sacred to Demeter and Kore, because it was where the first seeds were planted. The day called for daytime fasting, but in the evening women gathered together to eat. Dough models of snakes and male genitalia were buried to be dug up during the later Thesmophoria festival, which celebrated the harvest. Have a go at baking bread in these shapes yourself. ***Carol Tierney***

23. Make Offerings for the Spirits of the Land: Whenever you wish to leave an offering, consider the impact it might have on the place you leave it. Food and drink that biodegrade can help nourish the land and so are good for nature spirits, but dark chocolate might be eaten by animals and harm them. Coins are good as offerings at wishing wells, but bread would go mouldy! Choose a suitable offering for the spirits of the land around you and leave it out for them today. *Halo Quin*

24. International Fairy Day: Faery spirits are the embodiment of wild magic, they have a lot to teach us about reconnecting to the land. Through strengthening that connection we heal ourselves and the rifts between our world and theirs, allowing more magic and wonder through. Visit or make a space that feels fae-like to you. Make an offering in friendship. Breathe deeply, relax and feel the magic of the place. Choose something to wear in their honour that reminds you of the magic and enchantment of the wild world. Ask them to bless it for you. *Halo Quin*

25. Build on Relationships Started: Leave offerings and continue to wear the charm the fae blessed for you yesterday to encourage a re-enchantment of the world. Be aware of moments of connection and let them charge your charm. When you need it, you can call on this enchantment to lift you again. *Halo Quin*

26: Poem for the Day:

> *Summer*
> *Incandescent,*
> *heat that's stifling.*
> *Sweat pooling,*
> *in odd places.*
>
> *Lethargy,*
> *takes its toll.*

I'm stuck,
banana lounging.

Lobster red;
The pain is
exquisite.

Caravan,
43 degrees outside;
Warning: Hot Surface!

Cool change,
rain and lightning;
but thunder
scares the cat.

Sleep,
is a pipe-dream,
that blows in,
with the wind.
Ronin Shaman

27. Write Your Own Prayer: It could be an expression of gratitude, or intention. It could be a request, or expression that you are willing to hear from the divine. It doesn't have to be poetic, and you don't have to direct it anywhere in particular. If you work with deities, write something for them. If not, offer your prayers to the land or the universe and know that offering your own words is powerful. **Nimue Brown**

28. Poem for the Day:

Priestess
On desert at hilltop she stands

Open to the energies of the land
North and east, south and west,
She is balanced and blessed.
Eyes closed, mind open
Whilst the world around her sleeps,
She breathes in deep
The scent of sacred herbs.
She hears the distant sounds
Of animals, as words.
The silver Moon shines bright
Illuminating her as a Goddess of the night.
In silent meditation she stays
To hear what the Lord and Lady say.
Arietta Bryant

29. Feast Day in Honour of Papa Legba: Papa Legba is the gatekeeper to the spirit world in Voduo. He is also associated with the Sun as a life-giver and also the one to go to for matters of sex. Petition Papa Legba to remove any obstacles that are getting in your way and to provide new opportunities for your life then leave him an offering of sweets, cigars, rum or tobacco. **Rachel Patterson**

30. Spell to Cut Through Red Tape: Try this if you are struggling with bureaucracy. Get some red tape or ribbon of natural material. Cut a length to represent the problem. Then, cut that length into little pieces while visualising each element of the bureaucratic problem being resolved. When you have finished, put the bits in your compost bin, or bury them in your garden, where they will rot away. **Lucya Starza**

July

July's Moon is called the Buck Moon, according to some Pagan traditions, because it is the time when buck deer's antlers first start to show in preparation for the rut in autumn. Another traditional name is Hay Moon, because the full Moon shines at the start of the harvest. Consider what in your own life is ready to be harvested and what you might need to prepare for later in the year. Do rituals of celebration, get out and enjoy the glory of summer.

Leo the lion shines down in the heat of the Sun, which in astrology it enters from around July 22. It is a fire sign representing dignity, strength, confidence and power. Perform magic to bring these aspects into your life. The Sun moving into Leo can also bring new possibilities in situations that seemed hopeless.

1. Celebrate the Sun: We are past midsummer and all should be sunny and warm. Celebrate the joy of being alive, go outside, revel in the Sun and warmth, enjoy the light and the feel of the Sun on your closed eyelids. If the weather is not conducive to this – for example, in the UK it often rains in the summer – do this in meditation instead. Your energy is close to its highest and all is well with the world, even if it is not in your own life. Take time to forget your worries, remember obsession is the enemy of enlightenment. *Brendan Howlin*

2. Raidho Rune Lore: July 2nd is the midpoint of the year, 182 days before and after the New Year. This makes it an excellent time to consider where you are and whether you need to make any changes in your life. If you find you aren't making the progress you need, Raidho is the rune of movement and can be invoked to help you on your way. Research what it looks like, then wear it on an amulet or paint it in oil. It will help keep things moving. *Carol Tierney*

3. Get a Chinese Writing Stone: This stone is not only a full-body healing stone, but it also helps you adjust to change, is used to access information and stimulates thinking and creativity. It is the perfect stone for the ardent writer. This is a great day for writing poetry. According to some folklore, faeries have stones like this in their glens, as faeries love poetry. *Ravenwings*

4. Independence Day and Old Midsummer's Eve: While those in the United States are celebrating the nation's holiday with fireworks and fun, in some parts of England Old Midsummer's Eve is still honoured with bonfires or 'bales', which is a Saxon word for fire. Wherever you are, this is a good day for celebrating. *Lucya Starza*

5. Initiation into Magick and Your Personal Path: You don't need to make an oath to anyone else to be a magickal being. You only need to make a promise to yourself and to the deities you worship, to initiate yourself on a personal path. Speak honestly and with intent:

> *To the divine ones, I make a sacred promise.*
> *To the ancient ones, I will strive to know your names.*
> *[Your name] is a child of the stars and the keeper of mysteries.*
> *Know my heart is pure and my heart is open.*
> *Blessed be.*
> *Irisanya*

6. Make St John's Wort Infused Oil: Harvest the flowering tops of St John's wort and let them wilt for 6-24 hours. This allows moisture to evaporate and insects to leave. Place in a clean glass jar, leaving some headspace. Cover the petals with olive oil by about an inch. Place the lid on the jar tightly and set on a sunny windowsill for 4 weeks. Open every day and wipe out any condensation. Your oil will turn red from the medicinal constituents of the herb infusing into the oil. After a month, strain out the herbs. You can use St John's wort infused oil on its own or to make healing salves. *Jacqui Apostolides*

7. Herbal Infused Honey:

Fresh herbs (lavender, rose or thyme are good)
Jar with lid
Honey

Lightly pack jar with herbs, pour honey over the top, stopping to stir. When all the plant material is covered, give it another stir and leave for 2-4 weeks, stirring every couple of days. You can leave softer plant parts, like rose petals, in the honey, but strain tough parts out through a sieve. Gently warm the jar with the infused honey in before you strain it to help get the most honey out of the plant material. *Jacqui Apostolides*

8. Make a Salve:

226g/8 oz herbal infused oil(s) (one or a combination)
28g/1 oz beeswax or carnauba wax
Vitamin E oil
10-20 drops essential oil of choice (optional)
Jars or tins

Place oils and beeswax over a double boiler, gently warm over low heat until wax melts. Remove from heat, add essential oils and vitamin E oil. Quickly pour into prepared containers and cool completely. Stored in a cool location, they may last for 2 years. *Jacqui Apostolides*

9. Day of Remembrance for Unn the Deep Minded – An American Asatru Holiday: Also called Audh, she was one of the original settlers of Iceland. Although she did not remain heathen all her life, today she is honored for being renowned as a great and wise leader. She was a woman chieftain who taught her daughters and granddaughters to be great peace weavers. She freed slaves, forged international alliances and was buried in her longship. *Erin Lale*

10. Reach Out and Touch a Green Leaf: Feel the heat of the summer in the leaf. Allow yourself to resonate with that heat. Fill yourself up with abundance, with growth. Feel how you expand larger. Reach out to the leaf again. Connect to the life in the plant; to the connection it has to the Earth. Do you feel it touching you back? Send it love and go on your way. It will send love back. *Annette Wagner*

11. Feast Day of the Egyptian God Min: This ancient deity of fecundity dates back to prehistoric times. His whose emblem was the lettuce, which was believed to be an aphrodisiac. The Greeks identified him with Priapus. Serve a green salad with plenty of lettuce and help the God celebrate his feast day! *Mélusine Draco*

12. Feast Day of St John Gaulbert, Patron of Foresters, Park Rangers and Parks: For Pagans as well as Christians, this is a good day to walk in your local woods or, if in town, the nearest park. Take plenty of birdseed to honour the denizens of the place. *Mélusine Draco*

13. John Dee's Birthday: Dr John Dee was an Elizabethan scholar, mystic and owner of a large library. He didn't have the visions or voices normally associated with magical experience, but was a rational man. He linked science and magic, but suffered perse-cution because of his interest in magic. It is said that he succeeded in making gold from base metals, i.e. the mystical marriage that we should all strive for. Remember that one doesn't need flamboyant experience to be spiritually enlightened; living a good life is enough. *Brendan Howlin*

14. Roman Mercanus: This began six days of markets and fairs in Roman times. Use it as an opportunity to sort out all those unwanted items and take them to a local car-boot (yard) sale, offer them on internet, or donate them to charity. *Mélusine Draco*

15. St Swithin's Day: British folklore says if it rains on St Swithin's Day, it will rain for 40 days more.

> *St Swithun's day if thou dost rain*
> *For forty days it will remain*
> *St Swithun's day if thou be fair*
> *For forty days 'twill rain nae mare*

A variant goes:

> *If on St Swithun's day it really pours*
> *You're better off to stay indoors.*

Dry weather spell: Draw or colour in a picture of the Sun shining over a bright landscape and visualise it happening for real. *Lucya Starza*

16. Day of Erzulie Dantor: A Vodoun Goddess of love and women, Erzulie Dantor is a fierce warrior mother and a sensual lover, but can also turn into a strong and powerful crone. She channels all of the emotions from seduction to sobbing. Work with her for abundance, love, prosperity and passion. She will bring your life back on track if you ask for her help. Erzulie loves

perfume and sparklies – put on your finery today in her honour.
Rachel Patterson

17. Holiday Magic: Many of us take holidays by the sea or near some water. Here is a little bit of water magic to cast while you're away: Pick up one large pebble and one small pebble. Hold the larger stone placing into it all the negativity in your life currently. Cast this into the water. Hold the small stone and whisper into it things you want in life. Charge it in the water and carry it with you. *Jenny Cartledge*

18. Poem for the Day:

> *Mother Moon*
> *I never feel more strong in spirit*
> *More calm in mind*
> *More peaceful in body*
> *Than when I walk under the light*
> *Of a brightly shining Moon.*
> *Her beauty washes me clean of worry*
> *She peels away the shell of self-doubt*
> *Her presence comforts me*
> *And the night is my friend I seek her out whenever I am unsure*
> *No matter how wrong the day has gone*
> *My Mother the Moon leads me home.*
> **Ronikka Hubert**

19. Start of the Egyptian New Year: *'The Opening of the Year and the Feast of every God. The birth and feast of Re-Harakhte; ablution [purification] throughout the entire land in the water of the beginning of the High Nile [Inundation] which comes forth as fresh as Nun [the Chaos of Creation, or beginning]. And so, all Gods and Goddesses are in great festivity on this day and everybody likewise. Do not navigate ships or anything that goes on the water on this day.'* Extract from the

Cairo Calendar, No 86637, Cairo Museum. Honour the Deities of Ancient Egypt with a celebration on dry land. *Mélusine Draco*

20. Diktynna, Lady of the Nets: This is a good time of year for fishing. Whether you want to catch actual fish or something more figurative (prosperity, romance, health) you can call on the Minoan Goddess Diktynna to help you. Write down your desire in a few words then wrap the paper in a net. Ask Diktynna to help you land your catch then pour out a libation of salt water to her in thanks. *Laura Perry*

21. Roman Lucaria: A day sacred to Concordia, the Roman Goddess of concord or peace. Offer up a libation for peaceful solutions to the world's discord. *Mélusine Draco*

22. Feast of Mary Magdalene: An elevation of the Bride of Christ and the Black Madonna, Mary Magdalene received her own feast day from the Pope. Pagans remember she is another face of Isis who mourns, mothers and creates magic. Mary Magdalene heals our wounded psyche. Today, gaze into a hand mirror eye to eye. Say: '*This is enough, my pain ends here,*' as often as it takes to make it true. Send love to your image. Receive it in your heart. Make a gift to a women's shelter. *Dorothy Abrams*

23. Neptunalia: Honouring the Roman Neptunalia on this day would encourage ample rainfall for the crops and prevent drought. Neptune was an old Italian sea God and, as his festival falls at the height of summer, booths of foliage were erected to protect worshippers from the Sun. A perfect day for a summer garden party to make sure there's enough rain to water the flowers and vegetables. *Mélusine Draco*

24. Feast Day of Vatiaz: Vatiaz is a Mongolian Goddess and her buzzword is 'vitality'. Think about your own vitality. What makes you feel alive? If you can do it today, you should! Take some of the power of Vatiaz into you by creating a fresh green salad. Add other fruits or vegetables using all the colours of the rainbow – tomatoes, carrots, peppers, beetroot... (You might need to use edible flower petals for blue.) Visualise the health, strength and power of Vatiaz flooding into your food. Make a dressing with olive oil, lemon juice and marjoram, then find a sunny spot to sit and enjoy! *Arietta Bryant*

25. Furrinalia: This Roman celebration of feasting and drinking appears to date back to Etruscan times, in honour of an early-Italian Earth Goddess, with music and games as part of the celebrations. Another opportunity for al fresco entertaining as a cover for celebrating the forthcoming bounty from your garden. Offer wine mixed with spring water as a libation. *Mélusine Draco*

26. Feast Day of all Egyptian Gods and Goddesses: This was an ancient public holiday. Share an offering and join the celebration. *Mélusine Draco*

27. Sing: Make the time to sing something today. If you really can't use your voice, use a drum and make sound or vibrations. Give yourself permission to express yourself. Sing something that uplifts and inspires you – even if it's just a chorus. If you don't know a whole song by heart, commit to learning one. Most people can sing, if they put in the time, and songs are always soulful. *Nimue Brown*

28. Plant a Prayer Honoring the Dark Fertility God, Crom Dubh: The Irish festival Domhnach Crom Dubh was held on the last Sunday of July. Known also as Crom Cruach or Cenn Cruach, at this time of year the 'Dark, Crooked One' rises from the underworld to abduct Eithne, the corn maiden, and carry her away on his stooped back. Carve an ogham symbol on a bean and place in the ground to plant a fruitful prayer for the coming year. *Tiffany Lazic*

29. Ancient Egyptian New Year Feast Day of Wedjet of Buto: The fire-spitting cobra-Goddess' image was incorporated in the royal crown. This was the ultimate protective amulet. Reinforce the protections around your family and home – both physical and magical. Make a magical amulet from air-drying clay to hang in your front window, marked with a cobra symbol and the words: *'This house is protected!' Mélusine Draco*

30: Lughnasadh Bread: The day before, combine:

1 cup water
½ tsp yeast
1¼ cups bread flour
2 tbsp whole wheat flour
1 tbsp cornmeal

Let the dough sit overnight. Then add:

1 cup water
1 tbsp sea salt
1 tbsp sugar
¼ tsp yeast
¼ cup fresh chopped basil
3½ cups bread flour

Knead until it forms a ball. Cover and rest for 30 minutes in greased bowl. Place it on a baking sheet dusted with cornmeal, let it rise for 1 hour. Bake for 45 minutes at 450. *Amie Ravenson*

31. Ka Hae: Hawaii Day is celebrated to honour its flag. Honour your own tribal flag. Invite your close friends or family to a meal or tea party. Have craft supplies ready and a piece of cloth that will be your tribal flag. Design and create it together to put your combined energies into it. Covens and spiritual groups may want a symbol to represent their group. Choose when you will use it and celebrate your tribe and connection. *Rachel Mayatt*

August

This month is the busiest in the harvest season. Names given to the full Moon in August include Barley Moon, Corn Moon and Fruit Moon, reflecting this part of the agricultural cycle of the year. Even if we do not have fruit, veg or grain to gather ourselves, we can still make the most of the month. We can assess which of our plans and activities from earlier in the year have come to fruition and which of them still need more work.

In astrology, the Sun enters Virgo on or around August 22. This mutable earth sign represents a maiden with keen intellect who is also hardworking and modest. Virgo reminds us that the mind should serve the spirit, not vice versa. In Greek mythology she is Astraea, the last immortal to abandon the world when the Gods fled to Olympus. She is an appropriate symbol for the time when summer turns to autumn in the northern hemisphere. Make the most of the last glorious days of summer.

1. Lughnasadh: Also known as Lammas (Loaf Mass), this festival is named for the Celtic God Lugh. According to lore, Lugh was said to have been the inventor of the arts. Lughnasadh marks the beginning of the first of three harvest sabbats. Autumn Equinox (or Mabon) and Samhain are the other two. Lughnasadh marks the time when the sunlight is noticeably diminishing and the days grow shorter, the nights longer. The seeds planted at Beltane are now nearing maturity and will soon be harvested. Take time to think on what seeds – real or metaphorical – you have sown as the harvest is nigh.

This is a time to give thanks for the harvest and some refer to this time as the Festival of New Bread. Generally this festival is celebrated by the baking and breaking of bread. Light a candle and give thanks to the deities, decorate your altar with the fruits of the first harvest, make corn dollies, celebrate as you feel apt and drink in the warm rays of the fading summer Sun. The days will quickly grow shorter and colder; take time to contemplate what you will need to make it through the coming winter to ensure your larders are full. *Morgana Phenix*

2. Death of King Rufus: This marks the date on which the English King William Rufus was killed while hunting in the New Forest in 1100. Some say he was a Pagan sacrifice, others claim he was assassinated by order of his brother and successor Henry I. Numerous stories associated with his death include the account by William of Malmesbury, who recorded that the king's blood dripped to the earth during the whole journey, in keeping with the Pagan belief that the blood of the 'divine victim' must fall on the ground to ensure the continuing fertility of the land. *Mélusine Draco*

3. The Wag-Festival: This is one of Ancient Egypt's earliest-attested celebrations; it is mentioned several times in the pyramid texts. Wag is time to remember our ancestors and to re-establish our connections with them. This is a time for visiting cemeteries with offerings and prayers. It is time to make bread or beer and reflect on the cycle of life, of grape and wheat and Sun and stars and animals and people, the wheel is ever turning, ever changing, never ending. *Carol Tierney*

4. Aphrodite: Aphrodite reminds us to love ourselves, but we often don't make time for this in our lives. Today, take time to fall in love with yourself. Take yourself on a date. Write yourself a love letter. Pick up some roses to put in a place where you'll see them. Buy a new piece of jewelry (perhaps a pearl?). Go to the ocean. Sing songs to yourself. Hold yourself. Promise yourself and Aphrodite that you'll love yourself more fully. *Irisanya*

5. Official Start of the Oyster Season: It was once said that poverty and oysters went together. Beef and oyster pie was a traditional Victorian dish of the poor in England: the poorer you were the more oysters you put in your pie. Oysters were plentiful; the smaller ones sold as fast food on London's streets, while bigger ones were put in stews and pies to make up for the deficiency of meat. It was said that anyone eating an oyster this day would not lack for money for the remainder of the year. Try it! *Mélusine Draco*

6. Don's Day:

Don, our Mother, river deep,
Cradle us in summer sleep.
Hot, the days and bright the nights,
While Perseus showers us with lights
Of shooting stars, like seeds of life.
Hold us, Mother, free from strife.
You come to us when fields are high
With summer flowers about to die
And give us all their seeding fruits
To grow again into new shoots.
Mother, show us yet again
How life and death are both the same.
Elen Sentier

7. Feast of Cromn Dubh: Originally a pre-Celtic God of the harvest and the Underworld, Cromn Dubh walks the Earth accompanied by two black dogs. This suggests the origins of the diverse folklore legends of many large black, mythological dogs that have roamed the British countryside for centuries. Perhaps his ancient feast day is a good opportunity to give your canine companion a special treat in honour of the harvest, when dogs would have a field day chasing prey from the corn cutting. *Mélusine Draco*

8. Happiness Happens Day: It is a little known fact that today is Happiness Happens Day, when people worldwide celebrate being happy. This is something every self-respecting Pagan should get involved in because you can change the world by changing yourself and thereby inspiring others to do the same. Remember change begins with you and it is the example you set to others that gains respect. This is the main way in which other people will experience what a Pagan is or does. *Brendan Howlin*

9. International Day of the World's Indigenous Peoples: Today reflect on how many indigenous peoples have been pushed off their land and away from their ancient customs and traditions. The Western world owes them an apology and amends. Their wisdom can save our planet – if only we listen! Light a candle and apologise wholeheartedly to all indigenous peoples for any harm our ancestors did or we still do today. Next, meditate on words of wisdom shared by an indigenous elder. Remember: we are all indigenous! *Imelda Almqvist*

10. Recipe for a Purifying Sacred Bath: Salt is a deep cleanser on an energetic level and also good for aching muscles. Take one cup of sea salt and half a cup of Epsom salts. Mix together while picturing your soothing intent. Then add six drops each of frankincense, lavender and orange essential oils. Mix well. Add a cup full to a warm bath. *Rebecca Beattie*

11. End of the 'Dog Days': The end of the hottest time of the year and the drawing to a close of summer in the northern hemisphere. Celebrate the moment with a quite meditation on what you wish for yourself in the months to come and offer a libation of cider in payment. *Mélusine Draco*

12. A Story – The Ammonite Dream: When I was a child I had a fever dream. I dreamt I was an ammonite swimming in ancient oceans. When I died, my body sank to that primeval seabed, but my spirit lived, and remembered. Over aeons, entombed in rock that shifted and heated and cooled, I saw such wonders. Much time passed. The rock split and I fell as a pebble on a beach, cracking open to reveal inside my fossil. A child found me and wondered at me. Later, in a fever dream, I told her my story. Now she remembers, too. *(Ammonites are a symbol of the spiral of life.)* **Lucya Starza**

13. Festival of Diana, Mistress of Animals: Beginning on this date, for three nights, processions were held in and around Rome honoring the Goddess Diana. Their purpose was to avert storms that might damage crops perilously close to harvest. Like the Goddess Hecate, who was honored in similar ceremonies in Greece, Diana claims the torch as her symbol. Diana is mother of the light that governs the life rhythms of animals and plants. Light a candle to Diana and eat ripe grapes. **Hearth Moon Rising**

14. Second day of the Festival of Torches, in honour of Diana:

Cold modelling clay
A vervain or jasmine plant
An oak leaf

Invoke Diana, light three candles. With magical intention, make a small statuette of body parts that need healing. Say over them: *'Diana, I beseech you with this spell, with your light, make me well.'* Visualize her silver arrow enter the figure. Place them in soil with the oak-leaf and plant above, watering. Give thanks to Diana. Make small Goddess or deer figures with the remaining clay, place them around the plant as talismans. **Caroline Wise**

15. Japanese Ceremony of Toro Nagashi: This takes place at the end of the festival of Obon, during which spirits of the departed loved ones (the ancestors) are said to return; they are sent back to the spirit world in this sombre and moving ceremony of floating lanterns. Place floating candles and blossoms in a large bowl at twilight and sit with your memories – have a summer festival for the dead instead of waiting for winter. *Mélusine Draco*

16. Herbed Butter for Vesta's Bread: Vesta, the Roman Goddess of the hearth, emanates simplicity and humility. Her priestesses, the Vestal Virgins, kept the sacred flame alight, prepared herbs to sprinkle on sacrifices and baked ritual bread. Vesta herself was honored in every home, from modest to opulent. To hold family and community safe, combine these herbs (¼ cup total) with 1 stick unsalted butter: basil for protection, thyme for purification and a pinch of dill to attract positive energy. **Tiffany Lazic**

17. Portunes: The Roman God of ports, gates, harbors, fords, grain warehouses, keys and doors was often depicted on coins and ship figureheads as a two-faced being (much like Janus). During his solemn festival, Portunalia, keys were thrown into a bonfire to ensure good luck. Unlike most festivals, participants were somber – not merry. Perhaps this is because of the dual nature of Portunes, who ruled over both auspicious timing and inopportune timing – much like the unpredictability of the weather and the waves of the sea. *Janet Boyer*

18. Pendle Witch Trial: On this day in 1612, the famous Pendle witch trial began. Two days later, 10 were executed at Gallows Hill, in Lancaster, England, after spending months in a dark tower at the city castle. Their courageous story is full of shape-shifting familiars, clay images, stolen bones and even a 'gunpowder plot', but it stands as a chilling reminder to appreciate our freedom in today's society. Read up on this witch trial; I recommend Joyce Froome's *Wicked Enchantments: A History of the Pendle Witches and their Magic*. **Mark Anthony Terry**

19. Ganesha Chaturthi of Vinayak Chaturthi: Today Hindus celebrate the birthday of Lord Ganesh (Lord Ganapati) the elephant-headed God. The festival usually lasts for 10 days. Songs are sung and offerings made, usually in the form of sweet treats. He is the lord of good fortune, prosperity and success, but also lord of beginnings and remover of obstacles both material and spiritual. Ask for his help to clear the way for prosperity to pour into your life. Remember to leave him a yummy offering in return. To call his energy, chant: *'Om Gam Ganapataye Namaha.'* *Rachel Patterson*

20. First Light Altar: Get up before the dawn and find out where the first rays of sunlight enter your home. Create an altar to the Sun there. Hang some tiny bells, place Sun-loving crystals and draw sigils in lemon juice. Then, when you need to clear the stagnant energies out of your home, you can wake early, light some incense and ring the bells to draw in the glory of the morning Sun! *Mary Burkett*

21. The Magic of Lemon: The zippy scent of lemon can pack a powerful punch. Lemon can increase your vibration, lift your mood and cleanse your space. Each morning when you wake, put a tablespoon of lemon juice in a small glass or dish on your altar. Take a few moments to enjoy the smell and meditate. Focus on the positive manifestations you would like to see in your life. Try a lemon-scented body spray and put lemon juice in your bath. *Mary Burkett*

22. Paper Mache Guardians: Stretch a balloon over the small end of a funnel. Put in it your spell components, a few small crystals and some herbs or salt. Blow air in and tie the end. Then layer paper mache over it in an animal shape you like. Dragons are great guardians! Paint it and write sigils or runes; to make it pretty, add some glitter and glass eyes. Place guardians around your home for protection. *Mary Burkett*

23. Second Festival of Vertumnalia – Ripening Fruit: Vortumnus, Roman God of orchards and fruit, presided over the changes of the year. He was the husband of Pomona who he wooed in a succession of forms: reaper, ploughman, pruner of vines, etc. His name has been explained as coming from vertere – 'to turn' – as the God who changes shape and of the turning of the year (autumn, the season of fruits). Bonfires were lit in his honour and merrymaking took place – do the same. *Mélusine Draco*

24. Mundus Ritual of Ceres: Three times a year in Rome, a special hemispherical pit known as the mundus cerialis was opened with the announcement 'mundus patet'. Sacrifices and offerings to agricultural and underworld deities – especially Ceres, Goddess of grain and agriculture – occurred. The spirits of the dead were granted temporary leave from the underworld, a rare 'ghost holiday' when Romans made official contact with them. When discussing civil law, legal scholar Cato noted that the shape of the mundus symbolized an inversion of the upper heaven's dome. This is a good day to try to communicate with beloved ancestors who have passed on. *Janet Boyer*

25. Opiconsivia: Ops was the Roman Goddess of the wealth of the harvest and the purpose of this rite was to ensure the continuing fertility of the soil. Invoke Ops with offerings and with one hand placed on earth. *Mélusine Draco*

26. Feast Day of Ilmatar: A creation Goddess from Finnish legend, sometimes called Luonnotar, she is a deity of the air and created the world out of chaos. It is said she spent many hundreds of years underwater before joining with the air to create a child who arrived in the form of an egg. That egg fell, cracked and created the Earth and sky. As Luonnotar she is Goddess of birth and can be called upon to aid in conception and labour. Research other creation myths. *Arietta Bryant*

27. Inspiration: Make this affirmation: *'I open my life to inspiration. I recognise that inspiration can bless any part of my life, or any aspect of my work if I allow it. Everything I do can be done with soul, with heart and with integrity. I will be the best that I can be. I will do the best that I can do. I invite magic into my life to enable that. And when I am not all that I wanted, I will be gentle with myself, but not give up.'* *Nimue Brown*

28. Holiday Memories: On the last day of a holiday, find a small pebble as a memento. A stone with a hole is particularly magical. Stand in a beautiful spot with your pebble and say: *'Spirits of the land, sea and sky; spirits of place; I thank you for my holiday and ask your blessings. Let this pebble remind me of this happy time and place.'* Focus your happy memories into the pebble. Thank the spirits and keep the pebble with you. Hold it if you ever need happy thoughts. *Lucya Starza*

29. Midnight Muffins: This kitchen witchery should be done at midnight on the full Moon. It's a harvest celebration and spell to increase harvest rewards. Light candles and incense and draw a circle if you choose. Mix the following in a bowl or cauldron:

1 mashed banana
½ cup blueberry pie filling
1 cup applesauce
½ cup vegetable oil
1 cup sugar
1½ cups flour
1 tsp salt
1 tsp baking soda

1 tsp cinnamon
½ tsp allspice
½ tsp nutmeg

Bake in muffin pans at 325 for 25 minutes. Speak words of intent towards the oven while they bake! *Mary Burkett*

30. Habetrot's Day Eve: Habetrot, from the folklore of the northern borders of Britain, was associated with spinning and the spinning wheel, and had deformed lips. Her part in the tale was to spin linen to 'relieve unfortunates that caught 'grave-merels'(or 'grave-scab')', which was an illness causing trembling limbs, difficulty of breathing and apparent burning of the skin when the sufferer stepped on 'unchristened ground'. The linen itself had to be grown in a field that used manure from a farmyard undisturbed for 40 years. A niche-market indeed! Have a go at weaving or spinning. *Rebecca Bird*

31. Feast of Grapes: The ancient Minoans celebrated the grape harvest as the death of the vine God Dionysus, his sacrifice for the people so they could experience the ecstasy and joy his presence brings. Light a purple candle and pour out a libation of red wine or purple grape juice in Dionysus' honor. Think of the good things you have harvested in your life and the things that have brought you joy, and give thanks for them. *Laura Perry*

September

The full Moon closest to the Autumn Equinox is known as the Harvest Moon. The Harvest Moon rises only about 30 minutes after sunset, meaning that although the nights are drawing in, people out in the fields gathering the last crops can continue working under moonlight. This effect is noticeable for several days before and after the full Moon. You can make the most of the Harvest Moon for seasonal celebrations and outdoor Pagan gatherings too.

In astrology, the Sun enters Libra on or around September 22, the time of the Autumn Equinox when the day and night are of equal length. Libra is the sign of the scales, based on the scales of justice held by Themis, Greek Goddess of law. Perform magic to right wrongs and for justice to be upheld at this time of year. As Libra is all about balance, this is also a good time to work on collaborative projects.

1. Poem for the Day:

Mountain
Stone and earth,
reaching skyward.
White mantle,
shining.

Climbing over;
digging through;
living in;
because it's there.

Eternal vigil,
so we believe.

Gaia blinks;
the sentinel
recedes.
Ronin Shaman

2. Vine Month: Today marks the beginning of the Celtic month of Muin (Vine). It is a time of introspection, depth and balance. Sit before a mirror in candlelight and think of all you have accomplished in the past year, then think of what hasn't gone well. Scry in a black mirror, fire or smoke for a glimpse of what's to come. Write down your visions as messages for the coming year. Journal these experiences and leave a vine offering on your altar. **Jenny Cartledge**

3. Missing Days: On September 3, 1752, Britain switched from the solar Julian calendar to the more accurate Gregorian calendar, but this meant the date suddenly switched to being September 14. This is the start of the 'missing' 11 calendar days resulting from the calendar reform. Make the most of your time today, as time can go so quickly. **Mélusine Draco**

4. The Ludi Romani: The Roman Games were an ancient Roman religious event in honour of Jupiter. They originally ran from September 12 to September 14, but were later extended to September 19 and September 4, with the first day in honour of Julius Caesar. The Romans were also keen players of board games. Gather with friends to play board games with a Roman theme, or games our ancient ancestors might have played, in honour of the Roman Gods and Goddesses. **Lucya Starza**

5. Hungry Ghost Festival: On the 15th day of the 7th lunar calendar, many Asians celebrate the Hungry Ghost Festival, or Zhongyuan or Yu Lan. Buddhist scriptures describe many levels of hell (the underworld). This festival appeases restless souls who did not get a proper burial, were treated badly by family, perished violently or lived unhappily. In addition to offering fruit, meat, pastries and rice to these 'hungry' souls, celebrants also burn paper effigies of money (hell notes), cars, clothes, jewelry, houses, servants – anything useable in the afterlife (they believe burning joss paper will manifest the real items in the underworld). You could also burn joss paper – or incense – for those who died a tragic or violent death. *Janet Boyer*

6. Abbots Bromley Horn Dance: This English folk dance takes place in Abbots Bromley, Staffordshire, annually. Involving reindeer antlers, a hobby horse, Maid Marian and a fool, the custom dates back at least to the Middle Ages and some believe it has Pagan origins – possibly Anglo Saxon. September 6 is the earliest date it is performed each year. Learn about folk dances from your area or country. *Lucya Starza*

7. Day to Honour Yemaya:

> *Yemaya, mother of fishes,*
> *Combing your locks*
> *With pure siren song.*
> *Today help me honour*
> *the all-mother ocean,*
> *and let me do her no wrong.*

Yemaya is a Yoruban Orisha, Goddess and bringer of life. Her realm is the surface of the ocean. Wear something white, sing in the shower or keep an image of a mermaid visible in her honour today. Bless sea salt in a white shell for use in purification. Avoid plastics. *Halo Quin*

8. Nativity of the Virgin Mary: As the traditional day to celebrate the Virgin Mary, reconnect with your own representation of the

Mother Goddess. When part of the Triple Goddess, the Mother is represented by the colour red and earthy fragrances like patchouli; but use whatever speaks to you, magick is more powerful when it is personal. Bathe using your chosen Mother Goddess scents. Later, either robed in red or naked, sit with a lit candle and allow the Mother Goddess to connect with you. Connect with your inner Mother, connect with your own Mother and allow whatever emotions you feel to surface. Note images you receive. *Arietta Bryant*

9. Wonderful Weirdos Day: This thoroughly modern holiday for celebrating our wierdness was created by Tom Roy of Austin, USA. Let your wonderful inner weirdo out. As many modern Pagan witches say – do what you will, but harm none. *Lucya Starza*

10. Incense to Bring Clarity of Mind:

> 1 tbsp of frankincense pearls
> ½ tbsp of pine resin
> 4 bay leaves
> 1 sprig of rosemary
> ½ tbsp of dried mint
> 10 drops of rosemary essential oil

Grind the leaves in a pestle and mortar, add the resin, and finally the essential oils. Fill a censer with salt or sand, then place a lit charcoal disc on top. Sprinkle on the incense, making sure you keep the windows open and the room well aired. *Rebecca Beattie*

11. Halegmonath: The Anglo Saxons knew September as Halegmonath, or 'Holy Month'. There were feasts to honour Gods associates with agriculture, including Frey and Sif, and to celebrate the harvest's end. Share a meal with friends, with local seasonal produce. The rune jera means harvest or good year, wear it when you are working hard and want good results. This was also the time of the Völsi blót: The Völsi was a horse penis. It was taken from a stallion during butchering. The mistress of the hearth took it for her God, and kept it in a coffin with linen and leeks. On the night of the blot, the penis was passed around for everyone to greet. *Carol Tierney*

12. Personal Harvest: As we prepare to bring in our physical harvest, we can also take time to assess our spiritual harvest. What did you sow this year? What will you reap? Cut an apple horizontally so you can see the pentagram while reciting this poem:

> *Sour sweet juices*
> *To awaken my senses*
> *To nourish my soul*
> *As autumn commences*
> *I take into my body*
> *Fire, Water, Earth, and Air*
> *By the sacred star*
> *Hidden within there.*
> **Arietta Bryant**

13. Make a Corn Dolly: Corn dollies contain the spirit of the harvest. They keep her safe throughout the winter until seeds are sown in the spring, when she is ploughed back into the land. A simple corn dolly can be made by plaiting strands of corn into a loop, but you can also find patterns online for more complex, traditional corn dolly designs. *Lucya Starza*

14. Embrace the Dark: The nights grow longer and autumn's beautiful darkness creeps in – acknowledge this over the coming weeks. Align yourself to the season by spending more time in the dark – keep lighting levels low by using candles or small lamps to illuminate your home. Connect to the Earth's energies by cooking up big pots of vegetable stew. Realise the darkness is a reminder to slow down and conserve energy. Use the cold months for reflection and hibernation…then when spring arrives, you will flourish! *Mark Anthony Terry*

15. Poem for the Day:

Autumn
We yearn,
For a summer
that's not quite
over.

The barbie,
gets used less.
Footie rules,
cricket pulls
stumps.

Falling leaves,
like orange snow.
The raking
seems endless.

Urban umbrellas,
caught in the wind.
Ugly plastic daffodils
landing on
barren ground.
Ronin Shaman

16. Flying Ointment Recipe: Use at least five of these essential oils:

Parsley
Poppy seed
Mugwort
Sandalwood
Jasmine
Wild celery
Cinquefoil
Poplar leaf
Silverweed

Add 2 drops of each essential oil you have chosen to 50mls of sweet almond oil. Alternatively, use one part beeswax to two parts sweet almond oil. Place the beeswax and oil into heatproof bowl over a saucepan of hot water and melt. When it has cooled, add the oils and put into a sterilized jar. Keep it in the refrigerator. You can rub some of the ointment on your wrists. (From *Hedge Riding*) ***Harmonia Saille***

17. Birthday of Hildegard of Bingen: Hildegard of Bingen (1098-1179) was a visionary abbess, sometimes called 'The Sybil of the Rhine'. She wrote treatises about theology, medicine and music and was consulted by influential people of her time. She wrote about the medicinal uses of plants, animals, trees and stones. Today her writings appear surprisingly modern. From childhood on her visions connected her to universal wisdom and she prescribed many remedies for healing sicknesses of the human soul. Google Hildegard's name and try one of recipes, pieces of guidance or prayers. ***Imelda Almqvist***

18. Start of the Eleusian Mysteries: In Greece, the Festival of the Eleusinian Mysteries was celebrated on this day, and the next.

Many Romans sought admittance to these mysteries, including Marcus Aurelius, who succeeded, and Nero, who did not. Cicero, who succeeded, implied of the rites of Eleusis that '...they seem to be a recognition of the powers of Nature rather than the power of God'. *Mélusine Draco*

19. Grape Pear Crisp:

> 5 Bosc pears, peeled and chopped
> 3 cups green grapes, halved
> ½ cup red wine
> ⅛ cup lemon juice
> 2½ cups oats
> ½ cup flour
> 1½ cups brown sugar
> 1 cup vegan butter
> ½ tsp nutmeg

Combine fruit, wine, and lemon juice in baking dish, set aside. Combine the other ingredients in a bowl, mix with your hands, incorporating the butter evenly. Spread mixture over fruit. Bake at 475, covered, for 20 minutes, then uncover for 10 minutes. *Amie Ravenson*

20. Equinox Candle Spell for Balance: Take two sheets of paper, a pen and two candles – one black and one white. Light the two candles and make two lists – one of things you want more time for in your life and the second of things you want to spend less time doing. After you have finished, put your lists somewhere safe and keep up your good intentions. *Lucya Starza*

21. Fall/Autumn Equinox, Meán Fomhair, Alban Elfed: Make offerings to a sacred fire, such as dried herbs, whiskey, butter or ghee. Pour milk offerings on stones. Offer ale and oatmeal gruel to the sea. Pour ale, honey, cider or milk on the earth. Make a scarecrow from new grain and place it in the exact center of your field, allotment or kitchen garden. Do not give it clothes. The Spirit of the Grain will inhabit the scarecrow and look out for the welfare of your crops. Gather fresh herbs and hang them on a wall, keep them there until Samhain of the next year when they can be burned in a ritual fire. Fall/Autumn Equinox is the middle of the harvest; offer the first fruits, roots and grains you gather. The 'second harvest' is often hard fruit such as pears and apples, and a lot of vegetables, especially root crops. Have a harvest swap, bake bread, drink cider and a portion of everything can be offered to the spirits. *Ellen Evert Hopman*

22. Drinking your Intention: Take a cup of water and hold it in your hands. Think about the thing you want to change in your life and breathe that into the water. Picture a bright white light coming from the Moon, the Sun, or the stars. Allow that energy to plunge into the cup, transforming all of the negative energy until the cup feels like it's glowing. Once the energy has been transformed, drink the water and drink the changes to come. *Irisanya*

23. Fighting Post-Equinox Blues: For some, the Autumn Equinox can be jarring realisation that summer is over and that darkness will only get deeper for many weeks now. To combat any unwanted sadness, start a happiness jar. Clean an empty jar. Write down the last few times you were really happy on separate scraps of paper. Fold them and put them in the jar. Pledge to write down your joyful moments. On the days when you feel sad, get the jar out and read your scraps of happiness. *Mabh Savage*

24. Birthday of Edward Bach: Edward Bach was born on September 24, 1886. After finishing his education, Bach worked in his father's brass foundry. It was soon clear that foundry work was not for him so he followed his passion to help others and became a doctor. Through his medical career he worked as a pathologist, bacteriologist and homeopath before developing what was his life's work, the Bach Flower Essences. Bach intended the remedies to be simple and available for everyone to use. Intuitively pick or dowse an essence to help you today. *Jo Robson*

25. Enderi: Enderi marks Quellë the Elven Fading Season, and are the three 'Middle-Days' half-way through the Loa, the Elven year, set aside for rest and travel. This time aligns with Vána's husband, Oromë, Lord of Forests, the handsome, hound-loving hunter-warrior who blows his horn, Valaróma, riding Nahar, a white horse that shines silver at night. He loves Arda the Earth, and the Elves as they travel with him, inspiring them to make the sea journey to Valinor, the Blessed Realm. *Calantirniel*

26. Feast Day of St Cyprian: The patron of sorcerers served the Old Gods, despite being named a Christian saint. Research more about him. *Mélusine Draco*

27. Birth and Rebirth: Eileithyia is the Minoan midwife-Goddess who helps women birth babies. She also helps all of us birth ourselves into new projects, new relationships and new phases of life. Imagine yourself in her womb-cave, safe and warm. You have everything you need to begin something new. Now she pushes you toward the light, toward the cave opening and a wonderful new beginning. What will you rebirth yourself into today? *Laura Perry*

28. St Simon's and St Jude's Day: This traditionally marks the end of fine weather in the old agricultural calendar. Other weather folklore states that if there are lots of acorns on the oak trees at the end of September, it will be a white Yule. Go outside, have a look and find out later if the prediction is right. *Mélusine Draco* and *Lucya Starza*

29. Poem for the Day:

Autumn Arrives
Summer has fallen
Slain by the silent sword of winter,
Summer dies in flames
The trees ablaze with colour
Until the crisp winds blow
And the leaves fall
As a kaleidoscope of colour
Lit by the Harvest Moon
Jewel coloured leaves litter the ground
Summer is buried beneath
Autumn has arrived.
Arietta Bryant

30. Say Goodbye to Summer: Sometimes September can be very warm and give us an Indian Summer. Celebrate the day before the beginning of October as a time to say goodbye to warmer weather and appreciate autumn's beauty. Go for a walk if it's dry and collect a pile of leaves or beautiful shiny conkers to thread a needle through and hang in your windows for an autumnal blessing. Create leaf prints and cover notebooks or create gift wrap to keep for birthdays and other festivities. *Rachel Mayatt*

October

Unless it falls very early in the month and is a Harvest Moon, the name for the full Moon in October is Hunter's Moon or Blood Moon. The Pagan festival of Samhain on October 31 falls when historically animals and livestock would be slaughtered and preserved to provide meat for the winter months. It is a good time to honour those ancestors who lived by hunting or husbanding livestock, even if you do not eat meat yourself.

The Sun enters the sign of Scorpio on or around October 22. The astrological month of the scorpion often has a sting in its tale as the first frosts arrive in many parts of the northern hemisphere. It is a time for resourcefulness and planning, which this sign represents. Scorpio is also the sign of fundamental trans-formation – usually, but not always, for the better.

1. Older Persons Day: Young people in our culture often do not believe 'old age' will happen to them. Because we have become youth-obsessed we have lost a great resource: elders in our community who share wisdom, knowledge and traditions with younger generations. Meditate on the importance of elders. Find an elder tree and spend 15 minutes in meditation honouring the people who are (or were) elders in your life and helped shape your life. Send them gratitude! *Imelda Almqvist*

2. Arthur Edward Waite's Birthday: This is a great day to learn more about him or study his writings and translations, which include *The Pictorial Key to the Tarot*, *The Book of Ceremonial Magic*, *The Holy Kabbalah* and *Transcendental Magic*. Work with a Rider-Waite-Smith tarot deck for divination or magic. Meditate on the difference between fortune telling and divination. *Robert Scott*

3. Honoring the Spirits: The ancient Minoans revered the local nature spirits of Crete as well as the 'big name' Gods and Goddesses. Connect with the nature spirits wherever you live, even if that's a city:

I greet the spirits of this place,
The plants and animals,
Wind, water, and earth.
May you be blessed
With strength and vitality.
I honor you.
May we live together here
In harmony and peace.
Laura Perry

4. October Winds Bring Change: You can't avoid them, so embrace them! The days leading up to Samhain are about transformation – let go of stagnant energy and contemplate spiritual development. As the trees drop their leaves, shed in a similar way. Write a list of things that are stunting your spiritual growth. Are you stuck in a routine? Does a relationship leave you feeling constantly drained? On a second page, list things you'd like to attract. Use your mind's eye to imagine these changes taking effect. **Mark Anthony Terry**

5. Let Go: Collect fallen leaves and write whatever you intend to let go of onto them. Throw them into a river, or tear and scatter them into the wind as you chant:

A bind once heavy, a bind once strong,
By the will of October, bind be gone!
See it shrivel, see it shrink
As this bind and I unlink.

Acknowledge the water or wind carrying your problems away,

then actively work on ridding the nuisance(s) from your life. *Mark Anthony Terry*

6. Spell to Attract: Cut an apple in half horizontally to reveal a pentagram, then sandwich a list of things you wish to attract between the pieces. Bind the fruit back together with an orange or gold ribbon, then bury it deep in the soil. Know your desires now develop in Gaia's womb. **Mark Anthony Terry**

7. Honour October's Spirit of Reinvention: Doing something (safe) that pushes you out of your comfort zone. Drive a tricky route you stubbornly avoid, have a conversation you've been dreading or face a personal fear. Constantly putting things off will hold you back. Realise you are capable, and move forward! *Mark Anthony Terry*

8. Leaf Lore: According to English folklore, if you catch a falling leaf in autumn, you will be free from colds all winter. Another saying is that for every leaf you catch, you will have a month of luck next year. *Lucya Starza*

9. Divine Wisdom: Today celebrate the Goddesses Sophia, Minerva and Athena. Wisdom is the intentional integration and application of life lessons, knowledge and experience to challenges resulting in deepening awareness, recognition of the scales of balance and more optimism. Cultivate wisdom with sage tea. Sage is a harbinger of wisdom and a divine culinary.

   1 teaspoon dried sage leaves
   1 black tea bag (optional)

Cover the ingredients with boiled water, steep for 5-10 minutes. Add honey and a slice of lime if desired. **Jessica Bowman**

10. Crystal Gazing: Crystal ball gazing has been associated with divination and fortune telling, but is often misunderstood. Fortune tellers adopted many Eastern practices, some of which became mere decor. I was taught by a Buddhist monk for some time, and I asked about the crystal that was held by a Buddha statue. Rather than trying to 'see something', gaze into crystal ball or quartz crystal with the intention of clearing the mind and making the mind 'clear like the crystal'. This increases spiritual insight, clarity in perception and increased intuition. *Robert Scott*

11. Michaelmas Day: According to an old legend, blackberries should not be picked after this date. This is because, so folklore goes, Satan was banished from Heaven on this day, fell into a blackberry bush and cursed the brambles as he fell into them. As with all country sayings there is an element of truth since late in the season the fruit begins to spoil and the berries fall victim to mildew. *Mélusine Draco*

12. Aleister Crowley's Birthday: He was the founder of Thelema and the creator of the Thoth tarot deck. Regardless of your opinion of him personally, he undoubtedly had a influence on magick, Wicca and modern Paganism. Key written works include *Magick in Theory and in Practice, 777* and the *Book of Thoth*. Give an open-minded look – or second look – at his writing, listen to Mr. Crowley by Ozzy Osborne, and relate to him not just as a one-dimensional figure, but as a real and complex person. *Robert Scott*

13. October 13th and Friday 13th: The unlucky reputation of this day marks the anniversary of the destruction of the Knights Templar on Friday, 13th October, 1307. Keep a candle burning in their memory for as long as you can keep vigil and cast a protective shield around your home to keep everyone safe from treachery and intrigue. Prepare a decoction of bay leaves and when cool strain into a spray bottle and spray around the doors, windows, ventilation openings and the hearth repeating: *'By the power of the sword, keep me and mine safe from harm.'* **Mélusine Draco**

14. Wool Week: Magically, you can incorporate any intent into a piece you are creating, especially if the creation process is rhythmic and monotonous in nature, thus knitting and crochet are perfect for spellwork. Make a poppet, which is a magical doll. Find a pattern for a simple knitted doll. As you knit, meditate on your intentions, be they for a safe traveller charm or an aid to give up a bad habit, for example. Stuff the poppet with appropriate herbs – look up correspondences. Keep your poppet safe; squeeze to release the herbs' essential oils. **Rebecca Bird**

15. The Oak and the Acorn: Acknowledge and show gratitude for the abundance of the season. Symbols of the season include apples, pumpkins and the mighty oak tree. Reflect on the growth you have made from your acorn beginnings to the majestic and strong being you have become. Spend time celebrating you. Take a nature walk and collect an assortment of autumn leaves. Use leaves to press, make an art collage, or leaf rubbings. Let your imagination run wild. **Jessica Bowman**

16. Burying the Past: Find a dead leaf. Write on it – in non-toxic ink – something you wish to be rid of such as a bad habit or an addiction. Bury the leaf, saying:

Goodbye XXX,
You were part of my life,
But now you are dead to me.
I consign you to the earth.
May you rot there.

Let there be fertile ground
For better things to grow
In the fullness of time.

Go inside, have a warming drink and something to eat. *Lucya Starza*

17. Solid Ground: Collect some dirt from an outdoor area that is especially powerful for you. It could be some place in the woods, by a large tree, or maybe near some old ruins that you enjoy. Put in an urn made from natural materials, not metal or plastic. When you draw a circle for spellwork, place the urn at the earth station of your circle to add power to your spell. Keep it on the altar or sprinkle it around your home for protection. Blessed Be! *Mary Burkett*

18. Dark Moon Magic: In the energy of the dark Moon, it's a good idea to clean up your life. Clear away any unfinished tasks and physical clutter. You might also use this time to release old spells by either burying them or burning them. You can call on Hecate during the dark Moon. Call on her to help you find the right path to take now that the way is clear. Let her torches guide the way. *Irisanya*

19. The Fontinalia: This is the celebration of Fons, the Roman God of wells and springs. Wells and fountains were decorated with garlands and petals were thrown into the waters. Water is often overlooked, but it is one of the fundamental needs for life. Celebrate Fontinalia by donating to one of the environmental organisations fighting to provide access to clean water for everyone on the planet, and with your own water-worship, perhaps sprinkling flowers into a nearby stream or lake. *Carol Tierney*

20. Sibylla Name Day in Sweden: Sweden operates a calendar of name days for every day of the year. Some people celebrate their name day in addition to their birthday. In ancient Greece the sibyls were women who prophesied at holy sites and performed oracular work. The best known poem in the Poetic Edda is the *Voluspa* where a Völva (seeress, sibyl) tells the story of both the creation and the end of the world. This text remains a primary source for studies in Norse Shamanism. Google the Swedish calendar of name days and find your own name and special day or, failing that, the name that most resembles yours. *Imelda Almqvist*

21. Apple Day: This annual celebration of apples and orchards is a modern festival, although the Pagan festival Pomonia, for the Roman orchard Goddess Pomona, was soon after on November 1, marking the end of the apple harvest. It was celebrated with games that might have included apple bobbing. Eat an apple today – or bake an apple pie – in honour of Pomona. *Lucya Starza*

22. The Avalonian Cycle of Healing: This is a powerful tool for manifesting the authentic self and honoring the rhythms of nature with which we ebb and flow. Undertake this journey at Descent. Fill a cauldron or bowl with water and sit, reflecting on your life. What challenges are you facing? What is holding you back from happiness? Pour all thoughts and emotions that arise into the water and ask for a vision or symbol to appear on its surface, to aid you in your healing. *Lori Feldmann*

23. The Avalonian Cycle – Confrontation: Draw a nine-whirled spiral onto paper. From the outmost point, trace the spiral slowly inwards with your finger, thinking about what controls the thoughts and actions that feed your shadow. Why do you repeat behavior that does not serve you? What is the root of your pain?

Upon reaching the center, sit with what has come to you, before slowly spiraling back out again. Repeat two more times, each time reaching deeper inward for clarity. *Lori Feldmann*

24. The Avalonian Cycle – Emergence: Stand and visualize a door. On its surface, see the version of yourself you most wish for – one who acts from wholeness and center. When the image is clear, open the door and walk through. As you do, imagine becoming this sovereign, actualized version of yourself. Feel what it is to be them in every respect – breathe in their energy. When ready, step back through and close the door, while carrying this new potential with you. *Lori Feldmann*

25. The Avalonian Cycle – Resolution: To celebrate, horizontally slice an apple, symbol of wisdom and Avalon, revealing the five-pointed star. Remove the seeds and cut half the apple into five slices. Enjoy each slice, while saying something you love about yourself. Offer the remaining half to a favorite outdoor spot, thanking nature for its cyclic journey. As we celebrate harvest, so we see what lies fallow. Plant the five seeds into the earth, knowing once more the journey of rebirthing awaits. *Lori Feldmann*

26. The Avalonian Cycle – Integration: Feel the totality of your journey. Standing in your sacred space, take deep, slow breaths, and envision yourself as a tree. Feel your toes rooting into the ground. Raise your arms and feel your fingers elongating into branches. Envision the energies rising up from the darkness of the Earth, transforming and flowing upward into the lightness of the sky. Feel your body bridging where you have come from to where you are now, and settle into a feeling of wholeness. *Lori Feldmann*

27. Samhain Pumpkin Chili:

1 onion
1 tbsp vegan butter
4 cans black beans, rinsed
2 cans hominy, drained
30 oz can pumpkin
30 oz can tomato sauce
2½ tbsp chili powder
1 tbsp cumin
1 tsp pepper
2 tbsp salt
1 tsp onion powder
¼ tsp cloves
½ tsp cinnamon
1 can vegetable broth
2 cups beer
½ cup quinoa

Sauté onion in butter. Add all the ingredients except the quinoa. Simmer for 45 minutes on a medium-low heat. Add the quinoa, simmer for 15 minutes. *Amie Ravenson*

28. Lakshmi: This beautiful Goddess is celebrated throughout the Hindu festival of Diwali. The dawn of her celebration day is brought in with the sounds of bells and drums bringing her light into the darkness. She is a Goddess of wealth, prosperity, abundance, knowledge, skills and talent. She can manifest your complete spiritual and material wellbeing. Chant a mantra to ask for blessings from Lakshmi: *'Om shrim maha lakshmiyei swaha,'* which means: *'Om and salutations to she who manifests every kind of abundance.'* *Rachel Patterson*

29. Cat Day: Many countries recognise National Cat Day.

Celebrate our feline friends and honour the Spirit of Cat. Invoke the spirit of Cat into your daily life or for particular spell work. Among other qualities, Cat is blessed with amazing eyesight, agility and sharp claws! You could honour the Egyptian Goddess Bast and make an offering of milk or cream to her while asking for the blessings of Cat. In the UK, National Black Cat Day takes place in October to celebrate black cats, which often struggle to be homed because people consider them unlucky. *Rachel Mayatt*

30. Honour the Ancestors: In religions like Voodoo, Santeria and Vodou, the true spirits of Halloween are the ancestors. Festivities run from October 30th to November 2nd. There are dumb suppers, ancestor altars and offerings including rum, chocolate, coffee, fruit, cigars, cigarettes and other specific items. Pictures of those who have died are usually placed upon the altars. It is the time to honor, reconnect and remember those who have gone before us. *Ravenwings*

31. Samhain: October 31st is one of the most sacred dates in the Pagan calendar. In Celtic traditions, it is Samhain, the end of the old year and the beginning of the new. To people all over the world, it represents the time when the veils between the world of the living and the dead are at their thinnest, and is an ideal time to honour your ancestors, both familial and energetic (not all ancestors have to be blood relatives after all). In Mexico, families celebrate the Day of the Dead, while In Upper Egypt, people gather at family tombs and feast.

In Wicca, we give thanks for our ancestors, and honour the Horned God at this time. My grandmother High Priestess always referred to it simply as Hallowe'en, since she preferred her labels to come without fuss. In circle we bring mementos and place them on the central altar – photographs of ancestors, items that they owned, or just ourselves. We sing the songs we loved, read poems and share our memories of them. We draw tarot cards and use divination to understand what we need to focus on in the cold months ahead. At the feast we set a place for the ancestors and allow space for them to join us. We feel them draw near around us and ask them to help us with our challenges in the year ahead. *Rebecca Beattie*

November

One Pagan name for this month's full Moon is Mourning Moon, and November is a time to grieve for that which has gone before entering into the festive season of Yule. The nights are getting longer, the leaves are falling from the trees and the last autumn flowers are dying. Remember that it is okay to mourn, but also celebrate the memories that remain.

In astrology, the Sun moves from Scorpio, where it starts the month, to Sagittarius on or around November 21. Sagittarius is the centaur of mythology, a learned healer and highly intelligent, but also a brave warrior armed with a bow and arrows. This is about honesty and straight talking. Do magic for healing, wisdom or to champion a just cause under the power of this sign.

1. All Saints' Day: Known to Catholics as All Saints' Day, it is simply the worship of saints. The word for it is Hagiolatry (pronounced hag-ee- OL-uh- tree). It comes from the Greek hagio- holy plus -latry; worship. Saints are worshipped by practitioners of Santeria, Hoodoo, Voodoo and even Stregheria to name a few. If you are looking for a job you can always ask Saint Cayetano for help – he is the patron of the unemployed. *Ravenwings*

2. Baron Samedi and Maman Brigitte: Baron Samedi is a Loa of the dead along with his wife Maman Brigitte. They are head of the Ghede family of Loas, the largest family of Loa in Vodou who embody the power of death and fertility. They are loud, rude (they both swear…a lot), sexual and definitely know how to have a good time. The Baron can be found at the crossroads between the worlds and greets the souls of the dead as he leads them to the Underworld. Maman Brigitte likes to drink chilli-infused rum and swears just as much as the Baron; she guards graveyards and cemeteries. This day is The Festival of the Dead, celebrate your loved ones who have passed over...drink rum and eat chillies and ask for protection from the Baron and Maman Brigitte. You could even swear lots too... **Rachel Patterson**

3. Sun in Scorpio: In astrology the Sun rules this part of the Zodiac ; the light may be weakening, yet the Sun now is powerful. Go out of your home, greet the Sun and say: '*As autumn unfolds, there is no need to despair. The new Sun at midwinter is calling us softly.*' Then go in and ponder your possibilities; they are more reasonable than you sometimes fear. **Hennie van Geel**

4. Bonfire Night Eve Animal Protection: Everywhere in England, fireworks are going off. It's a nightmare for cats and dogs, and deadly for foxes, hedgehogs and other wild animals. Make sure you keep your cats in at this time of year, including letting visitors know not to let the cat out. Check any bonfire piles for hedgehogs, and maybe leave a dish of suitable food out to encourage them away from danger. Whisper this chant at your door or window:

Cernunnos be their guide
Herne be their courage
My words be their lifeline
All creatures be safe this night.
Mabh Savage

5. Bonfire Night/Guy Fawkes Night: Guy Fawkes Night is the celebration of failed terrorism (or rebellion) and since 1605 when the gunpowder plot was foiled, fires have been lit in celebration of the king being saved. As long as your animals are safe indoors, you can enjoy the fires too. Make some parkin, wrap some potatoes in foil, stick them in the fire and do a big pot of soup to share. As Pagans, we can see the fires as a way to illuminate the darkness as we approach the Winter Solstice, and as that promise of the Sun's inevitable return. *Mabh Savage*

6. Winds of Change: Be aware of the winds of change in your soul, your spirit, your mind and your physical world. Earth darkens, but in time the seasons will turn and the lands will be lit again with the coming of the first signs of spring. Prepare a heavy meal and enjoy the gifts of life while your thoughts are on what you are eating, every bite, every taste of the richness of your world. *Hennie van Geel*

7. Storm of Fears: Although sometimes the world is all turmoil and problems, not all is lost... Storm may abound, but life is strong. So are you and the ones you love. Bring yourself at ease and speak out your fears. Don't be shy, speak up, speak out and even give thanks. After that, relax and enjoy company. Maybe turn this day into a party, a feast, a ceremony under the sign of the fullness of friendship. *Hennie van Geel*

8. Lighting the Twin Flame: Many ancient cultures honored the dance of masculine and feminine reflected in a single deity. Greek Hermaphroditus became one with a nymph. Norse Ymir created the Earth from flesh and bone. Aztec Ometeotl reflected that creation is born out of the dance of opposites, giving birth to four sons, the four elemental directions. In honor of Intersex Day of Remembrance, light two candles, one black and one white, connecting with each side of your own dual nature. *Tiffany Lazic*

9. Social Justice: Remembering the ancient festival of Divine Justice inspires us to take action and start a revolution. We all have a responsibility to peacefully address the social justice issues of our time. Be a change agent and organize an activity to promote an important cause, pick up trash in your local park, or share information on social media to raise awareness. Get creative and promote peace. Even the smallest form of activism can make all the difference in the world. *Jessica Bowman*

10. Look Inside: Today some things might come to a close, but don't worry if they do, there are better times ahead. Sit by the fire, or burn a candle, weighing your options. Looking inside might be scary, yet every now and then one has to reflect on the things one really wants to accomplish, the things still on hand, and the things that have been. You will be happy, once you have gone through the process. *Hennie van Geel*

11. Old style Samhain, Lá Samhna, Calan Gaeof (Julian Calendar): Offer to fire: whiskey, butter, ghee, rosemary, a bunch of wild herbs collected over the year that has gone. Invoke The Morrígan. Leave a dish of the feast for the ancestors. Pour red wine, honey, cider or milk in fields and on stones. Offer ale and oatmeal gruel to the sea. Leave a little of the harvest in fields, below a tree and in the water. *Ellen Evert Hopman*

12. Feast of Thoth, Egyptian God of Writing, Wisdom and Magic: Make a libation of wine in his honour if you require assistance in these matters. *Mélusine Draco*

13. Cranberry Sparkle Cake: Spark up the holiday cheer; light cranberry scented candles and put on some feel good music, then dance your way clockwise through your home, sprinkling salt along the way! Then mix 1 box of white cake mix with 1 cup 7up or Sprite, and ½ cup thawed cranberry juice concentrate. Bake 350 for 30 minutes in two round cake pans. While it's baking, whisper your desires for the coming cycle towards the oven. Cool, frost and enjoy! Blessed Be! *Mary Burkett*

14. The Feast of Dionysus: Dionysus is known as the God of wine as well as the grape harvest and fertility. Celebrate this with rebelling against cooking! Have an appetizer party. Grapes of all varieties, muscadines, strawberries, dates and nuts of all kinds. Cheese and small finger food items. I find meatballs a good addition. I like to make raisin cinnamon scones and thumbprint cookies with raspberry jam for the center. Don't forget the best part: wine! *Ronikka Hubert*

15. Feast of St. Margaret of Scotland (aka Margaret of Wessex): Think about peace. What we imagine we can create. Sit quietly and send out images of international co-operation, love and tolerance. In 1969 in Washington DC 250,000-plus people peacefully demonstrated in against the Vietnam War in the Moratorium against War. Pete Seeger led the crowd singing Give Peace a Chance. That war ended – eventually. Too many others continue. Light a candle for peace and sing with as many of your friends as you can gather. Sing John Lennon's song, Give Peace a Chance. *Dorothy Abrams*

16. Night of Hecate: Time to celebrate and honor the Goddess known as the Goddess of the Hags or Wisewomen to the Greeks. Typically this night is celebrated beginning at sunset by leaving a supper of mushrooms and honey, goats' milk cheese, milk and bread at a crossroads. It is said that Hecate blesses those who leave her an offering on this night. Incense recipe:

    3 pinches sandalwood
    2 pinches cypress or pine
    1 pinch peppermint

Burn this alongside your food offering. *Morgana Phenix*

17. Blodmonath: To the Anglo-Saxons, November was Blodmonath (bloodmonth) because this was when cattle were slaughtered to provide food for the coming winter. Cattle were a status symbol, and display of wealth. The rune for cattle is Fehu, wearing this will attract wealth and status. The Saxons believed you had to spend money not just accumulate it. *'Friends must gladden each other...givers in return and repeat-givers are friends the longest.'* Today is the perfect day to buy a thank-you gift. **Carol Tierney**

18. Discussion: A lot of discussion is not necessarily a bad thing. The words can take a great weight off your mind and even lead to awareness of troubles too long avoided. It can help if you find a way to praise life, Mother Earth and deity, the Goddesses and/or the Gods. This is also a good day to connect with Otherworld and find or renew your role in Faerieland, Elfland and every kind of fairy-tale subtleness. **Hennie van Geel**

19. Onion Lore: A traditional weather proverb states:

> *Onion skins very thin*
> *Mild winter coming in;*
> *Onion skins thick and tough*
> *Coming winter cold and rough.*

Onions also feature prominently in many folk remedies, including for winter colds. So, cut up some onions and make a weather prediction – then make some onion soup to help keep colds at bay. **Lucya Starza**

20. Transgender Day of Remembrance: A day to remember those who have been killed as a result of transphobia. Light a candle in their honour and also research transgender Pagan deities, such as Dionysus of the Greek pantheon. **Lucya Starza**

21. First Day of Hrivë: The Elven Winter, and in the Elven Path this also marks Cuivérë Quendiva, the Elven Awakening in

Tolkien's stories before the creation of the Sun and the Moon. The sky was twilight color, with stars created by the ever-adored Star-Queen Varda Elentari. Helluin (Sirius) is deemed the star that actually awoke the Elves, the Star-People. They arose from the lake waters to look up and exclaimed: 'Eä!' (pronounced A-yah), meaning: 'Behold!' *Calantirniel*

22. Artemis: Sister of Apollo and lover of Orion, Artemis is the virgin huntress and the one who always does what needs to be done. A Moon Goddess, Artemis can also be a powerful ally during times when you might need strength and confidence. Take an eyeliner or marker and draw an arrow on yourself to help bring Artemis' surety into your heart and body. Leave the mark there until your next shower – and reapply as needed. *Irisanya*

23. Stir up Sunday: In England, the last Sunday before Advent is the traditional time to make a plum pudding for Yule or Christmas – a good pudding needs four weeks to mature. Make your favourite recipe then let everyone in the household stir the mixture and make a wish. Silver charms can be put in the pudding: a coin for wealth, a thimble for thrift, an anchor for safety and a wishbone for luck. *Lucya Starza*

24. Brumalia: This Ancient Roman winter festival was similar to modern Christmas. The festival, which involved feasting, drinking and merrimaking, was in honour of Saturn, God of plenty, renewal and time, and Ceres, Goddess of agriculture. Bacchus, God of wine, was also honoured. The holiday started earlier and earlier over the years – much like modern Christmas celebrations. By the Byzantine era, it began on November 24th and lasted for a month until the return of the light at Saturnalia. Share a drink with friends, with the traditional blessing, *'Vives annos'*, or, *'Live for years'*. *Lucya Starza*

25. Poem for the Day:

Candle Flame
Flickering drop of gold
Held upon a pearl white chord
Bright, like a star in this dark room.
Fluttering, as if you wish to escape;
To jump from your waxy prison
To light up the room with your warm glow.
We look to you with awe and wonder
But we fear your hot destructive bite.
Arietta Bryant

26. Egyptian Book of the Dead: On this day in 1922, Howard Carter and Lord Carnarvon were the first people for 3,000 years to enter the tomb of Pharaoh Tutankhamun. Look up *The Egyptian Book of the Dead* online and learn more about Ancient Egyptian funerary rites and afterlife beliefs. *Lucya Starza*

27. The Feast of Ullr: This is an American Asatru holiday. Ullr is the God of the bow, hunting, winter, and skiing. His counterpart who shares his spheres of influence is the Goddess Skadi. Ritual: Lay out a feast on the dinner table. Raise a toast to Ullr. Thank him for the bounty of winter hunting, or ask him for protection while skiing. Invite him to join the feast, then dine. *Erin Lale*

28. Magic Fondue Spell: Invite friends round, make up some chocolate fondue and put it in a ceramic fondue bowl with a tealight under it. Before the candle is lit, everyone should carve their initials into the tealight. Light it and pop it under the fondue. Everyone should take it in turns to stir the fondue, while making a wish and saying:

Double, double toil and trouble,

Chocolate melt and fondue bubble.
Candle burn and grant my wish,
And serve me up a delightful dish.
Lucya Starza

29. Make a Winter Solstice Advent Candle: Get a long, red candle. Measure 21 sections on it using a ruler and mark them on the candle with a cocktail stick, craft knife or witch's boline. Optionally, you can fill the marks with a coloured candle-writing pen. Burn one section each night until the Winter Solstice. You can make a wish each night too, if you want. *Lucya Starza*

30. Witch Balls: The glass baubles we hang on Yule trees might seem just ornaments, but they hark back to a magical tradition to ward off ill-wishing. Coloured glass balls were hung in windows. Sometimes pins were put inside. Negative energy – or evil spirits – would be attracted to the bauble and get trapped. They were also called 'watch balls' – as you should keep an eye on them and replace or cleanse them if they become tarnished. Hang a glass witch ball in your window. *Lucya Starza*

December

An old name for December's full Moon is Cold Moon, because it is when the winter weather begins to bite. It is sometimes called Long Night's Moon because it is the full Moon closest to the longest night of the year. This full Moon is powerful because it is visible for a long time. It is good for spells of renewal or endurance and for meditating on personal spiritual journeys and transformations.

In astrology, the Sun moves from the sign of Sagittarius the archer to Capricorn the goat with the tail of a fish at around December 21st, the Winter Solstice. At that time, the Sun seems to stand still briefly in the sky before the light is reborn into the world. It is a time of endings and beginnings; of hardship and hard times, but also of joy and celebration – a time to gather with family and friends and to wish for peace on Earth and goodwill to all.

1. Aleister Crowley's Deathday (1875-1947): Tarot spell for opportunity: Light a candle and place the Magician card on your altar. Visualize your intention, draw a horizontal figure of eight; with symbols representing your desire inside the two circles. Retrace while chanting:

I place into the lemniscate
Opportunities to create
Harmonising magically
As I will so mote it be!

Carry the paper with you for the rest of the day and burn in the evening. *Sheena Cundy*

2. Rest: The Soul still grows in dormant periods. A winter's journey: Light incense and a candle, cast a circle and sit in the north. Call in the Ancestors and relax to the beat of a drum. Make your intention to meet the Winter Spirit for healing guidance. Allow the energy to flow through you as you retreat into the womb of Mother Earth. Listen with all your senses. Return and reflect. *Sheena Cundy*

3. Power of Three – Musical Magic: Take a walk in nature and exercise your vocal chords too. Use your imagination, let go of any self-consciousness, make up a melody and sing:

Up to the sky, down to the ground
Spin the magic round and round
Over the land, out to the sea
All I need now comes to me
As I will so mote it be!

With intention, movement and music, you become an instrument for magic. *Sheena Cundy*

4. Rhiannon Meditation: Say: *'Rhiannon, the Great Queen, sovereign and powerful. You stood unjustly accused…telling everyone of your supposed wrongdoing. You stood for many years with the saddle on your back. You told the story so many times until the truth prevailed.'* Take someone else's story about you off your back. Feel its weight and feel its pressure around your body. With a breath, remove it from your neck and notice the lightness. Feel your freedom as a blessing from the Goddess Rhiannon. *Irisanya*

5. Sinterklaas Eve: This Dutch tradition celebrates the patron saint of children. At Sinterklaas parties, initials made from cookies are given, first to the youngest child. This custom of eating letters goes back to Germanic times. Newborn babies were given a runic letter made of bread as a symbol of fortune. Schools in the Middle Ages used them to teach the alphabet, eating the letter was the reward for learning. In the 19th century, sheets were used to cover St Nicholas presents and a letter on top identified the recipient. Make Sinterklaas cookies using a spiced gingerbread recipe on Sinterklaas Eve. Shape the dough before baking. *Carol Tierney*

6. Feast Day of St Nicholas: In the Netherlands children receive presents from Sinterklaas (as we affectionately call him) on this day. He arrives from Spain by steamboat, accompanied by his Zwarte Pieten (Black Peters) who keep track of the behaviour of all children. Sinterklaas rides his horse on the rooftops to drop presents through chimneys. Adults and older children often celebrate on the evening of December 5th with pakjesavond (an exchange of gifts, rhymes and banter). Invite small children to leave a shoe at your house, fill their shoes with treats for them today. *Imelda Almqvist*

7. Time to Get Serious about the Holidays: Memories are the best presents ever so have a family conference and see who wants to see or do what, who would come along if they had to and if one doesn't want to do it, let them pick where you eat afterwards. World peace should be top of everyone's list, but a 10-minute phone call with an old auntie will give you Cosmic Team points. After you have rung one, you will have fresh news to carry on to the next – you get the idea. Arranging to collect someone, meeting at another's place and bringing all the glamorous sandwiches is easy for you and so much easier than getting the bus for them. *Geraldine Beskin*

8. Finish Fiber Projects (or Displease Frau Holle): In the upcoming 12 days of Yule, no fiber arts projects should be started and the year's spinning, weaving and knitting should be finished before the year is out. Unfinished projects suggest laziness to

Frau Holle, who has been known to punish lapses in work. Those who are true to their fiber craft are rewarded by Frau Holle with inspiration and the blessings of abundance in the year to come. Donate unfinished works and cleanse your tools and yourself at this time. *December Fields-Bryant*

9. Be Sageful: Sage and onion stuffing is loved or loathed, but make sure you have some for yourself at the big feast later in the month as it is special to Sagittarius. To become sage, to wear your wisdom lightly is good, so give yourself a little conscious boost by eating a little. Dry some and make smudge sticks for space clearing at various times. Make it your 'thing' if you want to so you can rely on it being close to hand and it will help you to make wiser decisions. *Geraldine Beskin*

10. Tidy Up: Is your home looking good? We can be so critical of it at this time as the decorations look bad put up over clutter. Have a sort out of things that don't have a proper space yet and find somewhere for them. There is no time for a real clear out, just tidy up. Bedrooms too, as this is a time of intimate moments and reminiscences. Print out some silly photos, don't do everything yourself as you will need your energy later in the month. This is no time for martyrs, but for gliding along like a swan while paddling furiously beneath the water. When did you last dance to loud music? Do it in secret, it is more fun than the gym. *Geraldine Beskin*

11. Yule Eve Sachet Charm: Every year at this time, make any 12-herb Yule sachet in a red or green cotton bag. Charge it with this charm said thrice:

From Mother Night to New Year's Light
Blessings on your family
By caraway and clove and bay

Blessings from Yule Eve to Eve
Rev. Su Windsong

12. Make a List: Plan for the upcoming Winter Solstice. Do you want to start new traditions? Are you going to create crafts such as wreaths, ornaments or a Yule log, or bake cookies? Get organized. Make lists of things you need to purchase or gather. Make it a family project where everyone can be involved. Make your own cards for the season too! *Ravenwings*

13. Lucia's Day: Legends of Lucia detail her gouged-out eyes that became miraculously healed, which is why eyes are her primary symbol. She's often shown carrying a plate with her eyes on it and Mediterranean fishing boat captains sometimes paint her eyes on ship's prows so they can 'see' as they navigate the water. Eye-shaped amulets called Los Ojitos de Santa Lucia are reported to ward off the Evil Eye. The golden trumpet tree (*Tecoma stans*), or Saint Lucy's Eyes, is sacred to her and contains psychoactive alkaloids. *Janet Boyer*

14. Rider-Waite-Smith Tarot Anniversary: Pamela Coleman Smith was a freelance artist who was commissioned to paint a tarot deck. Nowadays it happens all the time, then it was risky and radical. When she did it, the stars aligned as the mystical magician Arthur Waite gave her the job and directed her as she worked. Their genius was to make each card show the inner and outer meaning for the first time and so the world's best-selling tarot was born. The subconscious cannot deal with words, only symbols, and that is where the enduring power and delight in using the deck comes from. *Geraldine Beskin*

15. Sagittarius: Sagittarians are lucky as a rule – some are successful gamblers. Traditionally they are generous and spiritual too. All the world's great religions, whether they are the ancient Earth-based ones or not, have a festival of lights around this time. Go crazy with the candles, the strings of lights, and know you are linking up with everyone around the globe. Have one special candle you light with compassion in your heart for the families who have suffered this year and wish them hope for the future. Then give a surprise kiss to the next person you see and watch them smile. *Geraldine Beskin*

16. Listen: How does your home feel? Sit quietly and settle your breathing. Listen to the silence. Where feels neglected? Too associated with petty rows? Space a bit tight? Do you need to calm the colours down or boost them? Where are you pleased with? Does everyone's bedding need an upgrade when the sales start? Get lost in all the pluses and minuses, then return to the centre again, settle your breathing and come back to normal. Let yourself into your home and see what a stranger sees. You know what you can do now and what you will address in the New Year. *Geraldine Beskin*

17. First Day of Saturnalia: Today is the start of Saturnalia, a festival in honour of Saturn, Roman God of the bounty of the Earth, the Ancient Roman equivalent of Christmas. Yuletide is a combination of fun and deadlines. Let today be your kickback-and-enjoy day. Invite your friends to a party! Feed them a succulent pork roast dedicated to Saturn. Seduce the returning Sun with beautiful banks of candles reflected in mirrors. Have a sack of gifts for your guests. Let them pick what they want, inspired by the spirit of fun. You may be surprised by who gets what! Laugh. Dance. Love. Hold nothing back! *Dorothy Abrams*

18. Festival of Epona: Epona is the Gallo-Roman horse Goddess often linked with similar deities such as the Welsh Goddess Rhiannon. In statues she is shown seated between two foals, holding a sheaf of wheat or a cornucopia. As a horse Goddess,

Epona is linked to protection, but also to family, home and fertility. Create an altar to Epona to invite her energies into your life. Her colours are green and white and you can burn sweet grass incense. Add to the altar apples and sugar lumps as offerings and you are ready to go. *Arietta Bryant*

19. Yule Pie:

Filling
2 tbsp vegan butter
1 onion
½ cabbage, shredded
2 cans diced tomatoes
1 package veggie 'meat' crumbles
3 tbsp curry powder
salt/pepper to taste

Sauté onion in butter, add other ingredients. Cook until wilted. Spread over two casserole dishes.

Topping
9 potatoes, peeled, boiled
3 tsp garlic powder
1½ tbsp parsley
1 cup almond milk
⅛ cup nutritional yeast (cheese substitute)
½ cup vegan butter
salt/pepper to taste

Whip ingredients together, layer over vegetables. Bake for 40 minutes at 350. *Amie Ravenson*

20. Poem for Midwinter's Eve:

Dark before light,
Day before night,
Holly King you shine so bright.
Your berries red, your leaves so green,
The snow beneath, a silver sheen.
You hide the darkness underneath,
While we young humans make a wreath
Of flesh and bones that come from you.
We celebrate your rising powers
With food and song and winter flowers.
For you bring to us the new-born king,
Arthur, bright as raven's wing,
Dark as feather, bright as blood,
And white as snow, before the flood.
Elen Sentier

21. The Solstice Sabbat: Midwinter in the northern hemisphere, Midsummer in the south, this is a day of changing light. Gather your friends to celebrate the Sun. Begin in a darkened room with one lit candle. Breathe together and ground. Then abruptly extinguish the candle. In the darkness, intone: *'Behold the longest (shortest) night of the year.'* Be still until they feel the weight of the dark. Then quickly ignite one candle in a circle of eight candles saying: *'This is the returning light of winter.'* Proceed with the next seven candles naming the sabbats: the light of Imbolc, the joy of Spring Equinox, the passion of Beltane, the full light of Summer Solstice, the fading Sun of Lammas, the harvest of Autumn Equinox, the dark of Samhain's Crone. Pause after each candle to let the significance of the Wheel of the Year penetrate to the bone. Then share yellow frosted cakes or cookies and a beverage of choice. **Dorothy Abrams**

22. Turuhalmë: This is Elvish for the Yule Log-Drawing. In Tië eldaliéva, the Elven Path tradition, this meryalë (holiday) aligns with Isil the Moon (opposing Anar the Sun for the Gates of Summer). In the Middle-Earth stories of Professor J.R.R. Tolkien, in the longest hours of darkness this time of year, the immortal Elves would sit around a fire, telling tales of their own who were slain in war. Many examples are in the *Silmarillion*. **Calantirniel**

23. Peace: Midwinter is a time for family, which can often lead to strains and arguments in close quarters. To stop them before they start, burn frankincense incense in the hallway of your home, opening all doors so the scent reaches every room. Say:

> Let there be peace these coming days,
> Keep all disagreements at bay,
> Let the air be happy and light,
> May every mood be high and bright.

Ring a bell to seal the spell and clear the air. **Jenny Cartledge**

24. Christmas Eve: On Christmas Eve, many churches hold candlelit services, often featuring organ music, carol singing and dramatizations of Jesus' birth; the latter practice was begun by St. Francis of Assisi in the 13th century. His famous Prayer of Peace fits beautifully even within many Pagan paths:

> Lord [or Deity of your choice], make me an instrument of thy peace.
> Where there is hatred, let me sow love.
> Where there is injury, pardon.
> There is doubt, faith.
> Where there is despair, hope.
> Where there is darkness, light.
> Where there is sadness, joy.
> Grant that I may not so much seek to be consoled as to console,
> To be understood as to understand,

To be loved as to love.
Janet Boyer

25. Poem for Sun-Return:

Three days standing
Still as stone.
Sunrise steady
Still as bone.
Now you change, and now you move,
New horizons for to prove.
Watched for three dark dawns we did
As you raised up the night's dark lid.
Letting go and setting free,
Breaking bounds so we can see.
So the old year slid away,
With all we'd done, both sad and gay.
Now you come with rainbow horns,
On this, the morning of all morns,
To bring us forward into light
That New Year offers us so bright.
Sun-return, we honour you,
And feast the year that comes anew.
Elen Sentier

26. Boxing Day: This is so called because, in the UK, the wealthy would give their servants a 'Christmas box', which was a thank you for good service through the year. This rather classist and outdated tradition can be made a bit more modern and compassionate. Is there a food bank near you? Go donate. Volunteer at a 'feed the homeless' event. Take your old clothes to a shelter or a charity shop. Check your elderly or vulnerable neighbours are okay. Christmas and the Solstice aren't fun for everyone; be a light in the darkness. *Mabh Savage*

27. Molybdomancy: A Finnish New Year's Eve tradition is fortune-telling with melted lead. You need special equipment: lead, a special metal pan to melt it in and a bowl of cold water. Everyone takes it in turn to tip a little melted lead into the water. The shape it solidified into indicates what to expect in the year to come. If you don't have the correct equipment for molybdomancy, you can do a similar divination using melted candle wax dripped into water instead. *Lucya Starza*

28. Menlosa Barns Dag (Finland): Called Varnlosa Barns Dag in Sweden and also called Fjärde Dag Jul (the Fourth Day of Christmas). This day commemorates the Massacre of the Innocents by King Herod, ordering the murder of all male infants at the time of Jesus Christ's birth. In old Swedish the word 'menlös' means innocent and 'värnlös' means defenseless. (Part of Finland is Swedish-speaking). Now it has the more general meaning of honouring innocent and defenseless children all over the world in need of support and protection. Meditate on a personal way of reaching out to vulnerable children in our world and act on insights received. *Imelda Almqvist*

29. Rasputin's Death: The 'mad monk', a Siberian peasant named Rasputin, was never a monk, but a staretzs – an independent, wandering holy man. His charisma and reputation for clairvoyance and healing made him popular among society ladies. One of them put Tsarina Alexandra in touch with the unkempt, intense Rasputin, since her son, Tsarevich Alexis – heir to the Russian throne – suffered from hemophilia. Rasputin cured young Alexis and earned a place in the royal inner circle. Despite surviving multiple assassination attempts, the 'demon saint' predicted his own death and, within weeks, was ambushed and killed by Prince Felix Yusupov. *Janet Boyer*

30. Austin Osman Spare's Birthday: Born on 30 December 1886,

Austin Osman Spare was an English artist and occultist. He was a skilled graphic designer and devised the magickal technique of sigilization. Take a word for something you wish for. Remove the vowels. Turn the remaining letters into a pattern – that is a sigil. Write it on a piece of paper and charge it. Spare liked to charge sigils using autoerotic sex magic, but you can charge them in other ways too. *Lucya Starza*

31. New Year's Eve Folk Traditions: My Aunty May was a firm believer in the necessity of the first foot. She required a tall, dark man to step over her threshold just after midnight between New Year's Eve and the New Year. My dad did this every year, with me tagging along behind excitedly. If you go to be the first foot at someone's house, take coal, whiskey and a 50 pence piece (or similar value coin in other currencies). This is wishing the household warmth, health and prosperity for the coming year. *Mabh Savage*

About the Contributors

Dorothy Abrams, co-founder of the Web PATH Center, a Pagan church and teaching center in Lyons, New York, USA, is the author of *Identity and the Quartered Circle: Studies in Applied Wicca* and a contributing writer for *Paganism 101, Naming the Goddess, Witchcraft Today 60 Years On* and *The Goddess in America*. She is the scribe and editor of a community book *Sacred Sex and Magick* by the Web PATH Center (2015). She was a speaker at the Museum of Witchraft and Magic, Boscastle, Cornwall, in October 2016, presenting a paper on Ancestor contact through Web PATH rituals at Samhain.

Imelda Almqvist teaches shamanism and sacred art internationally. She pioneered a shamanic programme for young people called The Time Travellers. Imelda's book *Natural Born Shamans: A Spiritual Toolkit For Life, Using Shamanism Creatively with Young People of all Ages* was published by Moon Books in 2016.

Jacqui Apostolides is a qualified herbalist and runs Bewitched Botanicals at www.bewitchedbotanicals.com, making soaps and other body products.

Laeynarrie Auvresti is a solitary high priestess who has tried to live her life in such a way as to show her children it is possible to stay true to one's heart and soul. Love, light, strength and hope is her ongoing wish for all she meets. Her focus has been cleansing, healing, protection and luck energy work.

Rebecca Beattie is the author of *Nature Mystics* and three books of Pagan-inspired fiction. A regular contributor to Pagan Dawn and a blogger at Moon Books, she is also a PhD candidate on the Creative Writing programme at Middlesex University.

Geraldine Beskin of London's The Atlantis Bookshop is a dedicated occultist, passionate magical historian and bookseller. She zooms off here, there and everywhere around the world whenever she is asked to present her talks on various esoteric matters. Always busy, she still has time to live in the moment and be still – sometimes!

Rebecca Bird has been a practising witch since she was a child. She has several cats, three children and two grandchildren, all of whom have become used to her ways! She crafts, does spellwork, healing and fortune-telling in its many guises. She also runs gatherings, workshops, meditations and open rituals, as well as holding handfastings, naming ceremonies and funerals.

Jessica Bowman is an educator, author, artist and healer. At the time of writing, she was immersed in a dissertation about art, activism and Goddess consciousness. Her quest is the pursuit of women's mysteries, cultivating magic and seeking the sacred. www.creativityandthedivinefeminine.com

Janet Boyer is the author of *Back in Time Tarot* (Hampton Roads), *Tarot in Reverse* (Schiffer Books), *Naked Tarot* (Dodona Books) and *365 Tarot: Daily Meditations* (Dodona Books). With her husband, artist Ron Boyer, she co-created *The Snowland Deck* and *The Coffee Tarot*. Visit her online at JanetBoyer.com.

Nimue Brown is the author of assorted Druid and Pagan titles published by Moon Books, the graphic novel series Hopeless Maine and several novels. She blogs every day at www.druidlife.wordpress.com and quietly walks her Druidry in the Cotswolds.

Arietta Bryant is a Pagan celebrant, writer, and mentor. She was the founder of The Children of the Sacred Laughter and is the co-founder of the Moon River Wicca Tradition. She has authored several solo books including, *Ramblings & Rhymes* – an anthology of poetry; and *Circles of Sacred Laughter* – a book of seasonal group rituals. Arietta contributed to Moon Books' publications *Naming the Goddess* and *Pagan Planet*. She lives in Hampshire, UK, with her husband, two children and two cats. Find her online at www.facebook.com/Arietta.smallsongs/

Mary Burkett is both a hedgewitch and a kitchen witch, and has studied her craft since childhood. Mary enjoys baking from scratch and says that 'food is ritual'. Mary spent much of her life in the wilds of Alaska, and now lives in Pennsylvania with her husband and two small children.

Calantirniel, from Southern California, USA, is published in Moon Books' anthologies *Paganism 101* and *Pagan Planet* and featured in more than two dozen Llewellyn annuals since 2007. She has practised many forms of natural spirituality for a quarter century and is currently exploring her Irish roots. Professionally, she is an astrologer, herbalist, tarot card reader, timing expert, dowser, Reiki master, energy healer, ULC reverend, and flower essence creator/practitioner. She is also a co-founder of Tië eldaliéva, meaning the Elven Path, a spiritual practice based upon the Elves' viewpoint in JRR Tolkien's Middle-Earth stories, particularly *The Silmarillion*. Find her at IntuitiveTiming.com and ElvenSpirituality.com.

Jenny Cartledge is a solitary Pagan witch who has been practising on and off for the past 14 years, wandering down paths for Wicca, Druidry and many differing types of witchcraft before deciding to not follow a named path. She enjoys writing about many different aspects of the craft and her work.

Sheena Cundy is author of *The Madness and the Magic* (Moon

Books), *The Magic of Nature Oracle* and is a singer-songwriter with Pagan band Morrigans Path. She is a spiritual healer (Reiki master), tarot reader, teacher of spiritual development and horse-riding. She is an Essex, UK, witch who lives by the sea. www.sheenacundy.com

Paula Dempsey has been fascinated by British folklore and magic for many years. Her interest in the history of British occult movements drew her into writing for role-playing games, including *The Book of the Smoke* for Trail of Cthulhu. She juggles writing at night with working as a careers adviser by day.

Mélusine Draco is the author of numerous titles on traditional British Old Craft including the popular *Traditional Witchcraft* series published by Moon Books. She is also Principal of Coven of the Scales www.covenofthescales.com

Lori Feldmann sits on the Council of Nine in the Sisterhood of Avalon and her passion lies in writing and in bringing women to the Goddess and in circle with one another.

December Fields-Bryant is a Northern Tradition Pagan and earthly handmaiden to Frigga. Her magical life is blessed with inspiration from her little imp of a baby boy and her Viking blacksmith husband. You can read more of her work at www.Terrestrials.earth or on Twitter @TerrestrialsAK.

Hennie van Geel, aged 59, lives in the Dutch city of Eindhoven. He is a Druid within OBOD and describes himself as: '*A humble (I hope) seeker on the Path.*'

Ellen Evert Hopman is an herbalist, Druid priestess, and author of a books including *A Legacy of Druids – Conversations with Druid leaders from Britain the USA and Canada, Secret Medicines From Your*

Garden, A Druid's Herbal of Sacred Tree Medicine and other volumes. She lives in an oak forest in New England, USA.

Dr Brendan Howlin is a full-time research scientist and Druid. He has published two books on Druidry with Moon Books and contributed to several anthologies. He co-founded the Surrey Druid Grove and has acted as a tutor for OBOD for nearly 20 years.

Ronikka Hubert grew up in Los Angeles, USA. She has been practising for more than 20 years her own unique tradition. She is ordained, as well as a Reiki level II practitioner. She lives in North Carolina, USA, where she attends college.

Irisanya is a Reclaiming Witch, initiate, priestess, international teacher, and drummer, as well as an often-vegan, shapeshifter, shadow stalker, invocateur and Sagittarius devoted to Aphrodite, Iris, Hecate and the Norns. She has been published in *Paganism 101, Naming the Goddess, Pagan Planet,* and *The Goddess in America* and makes her living in California, USA, as a writer and magick maker. www.irisanya.com

Erin Lale is the author of *Asatru For Beginners* and other books, and created the Heathen Calendar and Slavic Calendar classical art calendars.

Tiffany Lazic is a registered psychotherapist and spiritual director with a private practice in individual, couples and group therapy. As the owner of The Hive and Grove Centre for Holistic Wellness, she created two self-development programmes focused on teaching inner alchemy and intuitive tools from around the world. Tiffany is the author of *The Great Work: Self-Knowledge and Healing Through the Wheel of the Year*. Visit Tiffany at www.hiveandgrove.ca

Rev. Su Windsong Leone is a teacher, wedding officiant and intuitive reader living in Raleigh NC, USA, with her sci-fi author husband and their furbabies.

Rachel Mayatt is the author of *Natures Children – Celebrating the Seasons in a Pagan Family* (Capall Bann) and a Lulu.com book, *The Silver Hearth Witches Workbook*. As well as studying for a history/archaeology degree, she blogs at Urban Witch in Somerset, UK. Rachel has been on her path for more than 30 years and now practises quietly as a Hedgewitch in Glastonbury while helping organise the Beltane and Samhain festivals of the Glastonbury Dragons Celebrations.

Rachel Patterson is a witch and author of numerous books on the Craft, including *Grimoire of a Kitchen Witch, Pagan Portals – The Cailleach* and *Pagan Portals – Hoodoo: Folk Magic*. She is an elder of the Kitchen Witch online School of Witchcraft and high priestess of the Kitchen Witch Coven.

Morgana Phenix resides deep in the woods of northern Maine, USA. She is a solitary Druid, a retired special education teacher, writer, budding herbalist, goat farmer, Reiki master and tarot card reader.

Laura Perry is a Pagan author and artist with a special interest in the Minoans of ancient Crete. She is the author of *Ariadne's Thread: Awakening the Wonders of the Ancient Minoans in our Modern Lives*.

Halo Quin is a storyteller and Faery Witch living in Wales, author of *Pagan Portals: Your Faery Magic* and creator (and ringleader) of The Goblin Circus. For more: www.aworldenchanted.com

Amie Ravenson is a long-time eclectic, intuitive, solitary, kitchen witch who lives in Lawrenceville, GA, USA, with her husbear Josef, three dogs and a rat named Stanley. You can find her at www.AmieRavenson.com, or look for her podcast, Bewitching Your Day.

Ravenwings has been a practising witch for 31+ years. She works mostly with earth, nature, kitchen, and faery magick.

Hearth Moon Rising is a Dianic priestess and a priestess of Ishtar living in the Adirondack Mountains. She is the author of *Invoking Animal Magic: A Guide for the Pagan Priestess* (Moon Books). She blogs at hearthmoonblog.com.

Jo Robson is a member of OBOD and lives in Bolton, UK, with her partner Frank and their dog, Mab and cat, Sunshine. She has previously contributed to the Moon Book publications *Pagan Planet, Naming the Goddess* and *Paganism 101* as well as several other independently published books.

Yvonne Ryves is the author of *Shaman Pathways – Web of Life*, writes a regular column Shaman Moon for Indie Shaman Magazine and is a shamanic healer, energy healer and artist living in Ireland. Yvonne is training as an Ovate with OBOD.

Harmonia Saille is a Hedge Witch and author. She is the author of *Pagan Portals – Hedge Witchcraft* and *Hedge Riding*, and *The Spiritual Runes*. Harmonia lives in Ireland.

Mabh Savage is the author of *A Modern Celt: Seeking the Ancestors* and *Pagan Portals – Celtic Witchcraft*. She also writes poetry and plays music, and loves foraging and getting lost in the woods. Find her at soundsoftime.wordpress.com.

Robert Scott is a professional tarot reader and can be found online at ArcanaAdvising.com. He lives near Cincinnati, Ohio, USA.

Elen Sentier is a wild wilderness woman at heart, from a long family lineage in the British native tradition. She lives with her cats, husband and a host of wildlife in the back of beyond in the Welsh Marches, where she writes magic/mystery/romance novels about and books on the British native tradition. www.elensentier.co.uk

Ronin Shaman treads the Shamanic path after having studied under the late Kenneth Meadows, author and renowned shamanic practitioner, in London, UK. He has had a few short stories published, two in a now-defunct Pagan magazine called Dragonswood.

Lucya Starza writes A Bad Witch's Blog at www.badwitch.co.uk and is the author of *Pagan Portals – Candle Magic*. She is an unashamedly eclectic witch who lives in London, UK, and loves to have friends round for tea, magic and cackling.

Mark Anthony Terry is a hedge witch and writer who lives near York, UK. He has been fascinated by magick and witchcraft since he was a small boy. You can find him on Twitter using the handle @naja__

Carol Tierney is a re-constructionist heathen storyteller with an interest in the classics. She has written stories and articles for a variety of books and magazines.

Annette Wagner, M.A, says that her work in the world is about healing our connection to the Earth, which she does through Earth Prayers. You can view on these on Facebook as inspirational posts or on her site.

Caroline Wise has contributed to numerous books including *The Magical Writings of Florence Farr*, *Bast and Sekhmet the Eyes of Ra* by Storm Constantine, *Naming the Goddess*, *Eily, Austin Spare's Muse* by Dr William Wallace and *The Major Arcana* by Olivier Hibert. She also compiled the book *Finding Elen* and, with John Matthews, *The Secret Lore of London*. In the late 1980s to mid 1990s she edited the Skoob Occult Review, and also The Occult Observer when she owned The Atlantis Bookshop, in London, UK.

Moon Books

PAGANISM & SHAMANISM

What is Paganism? A religion, a spirituality, an alternative belief system, nature worship? You can find support for all these definitions (and many more) in dictionaries, encyclopaedias, and text books of religion, but subscribe to any one and the truth will evade you. Above all Paganism is a creative pursuit, an encounter with reality, an exploration of meaning and an expression of the soul. Druids, Heathens, Wiccans and others, all contribute their insights and literary riches to the Pagan tradition. Moon Books invites you to begin or to deepen your own encounter, right here, right now. If you have enjoyed this book, why not tell other readers by posting a review on your preferred book site. Recent bestsellers from Moon Books are:

Journey to the Dark Goddess
How to Return to Your Soul
Jane Meredith
Discover the powerful secrets of the Dark Goddess and transform your depression, grief and pain into healing and integration.
Paperback: 978-1-84694-677-6 ebook: 978-1-78099-223-5

Shamanic Reiki
Expanded Ways of Working with Universal Life Force Energy
Llyn Roberts, Robert Levy
Shamanism and Reiki are each powerful ways of healing;
together, their power multiplies. *Shamanic Reiki* introduces
techniques to help healers and Reiki practitioners tap ancient
healing wisdom.
Paperback: 978-1-84694-037-8 ebook: 978-1-84694-650-9

Pagan Portals – The Awen Alone
Walking the Path of the Solitary Druid
Joanna van der Hoeven
An introductory guide for the solitary Druid, *The Awen Alone*
will accompany you as you explore, and seek out your own
place within the natural world.
Paperback: 978-1-78279-547-6 ebook: 978-1-78279-546-9

A Kitchen Witch's World of Magical Herbs & Plants
Rachel Patterson
A journey into the magical world of herbs and plants, filled with
magical uses, folklore, history and practical magic. By popular
writer, blogger and kitchen witch, Tansy Firedragon.
Paperback: 978-1-78279-621-3 ebook: 978-1-78279-620-6

Medicine for the Soul
The Complete Book of Shamanic Healing
Ross Heaven
All you will ever need to know about shamanic healing and
how to become your own shaman...
Paperback: 978-1-78099-419-2 ebook: 978-1-78099-420-8

Shaman Pathways – The Druid Shaman
Exploring the Celtic Otherworld
Danu Forest
A practical guide to Celtic shamanism with exercises and
techniques as well as traditional lore for exploring the Celtic
Otherworld.
Paperback: 978-1-78099-615-8 ebook: 978-1-78099-616-5

Traditional Witchcraft for the Woods and Forests
A Witch's Guide to the Woodland with Guided Meditations and
Pathworking
Melusine Draco
A Witch's guide to walking alone in the woods, with guided
meditations and pathworking.
Paperback: 978-1-84694-803-9 ebook: 978-1-84694-804-6

Wild Earth, Wild Soul
A Manual for an Ecstatic Culture
Bill Pfeiffer
Imagine a nature-based culture so alive and so connected,
spreading like wildfire. This book is the first flame...
Paperback: 978-1-78099-187-0 ebook: 978-1-78099-188-7

Naming the Goddess
Trevor Greenfield
Naming the Goddess is written by over eighty adherents and
scholars of Goddess and Goddess Spirituality.
Paperback: 978-1-78279-476-9 ebook: 978-1-78279-475-2

Shapeshifting into Higher Consciousness
Heal and Transform Yourself and Our World with Ancient
Shamanic and Modern Methods
Llyn Roberts
Ancient and modern methods that you can use every day
to transform yourself and make a positive difference in the
world.
Paperback: 978-1-84694-843-5 ebook: 978-1-84694-844-2

Readers of ebooks can buy or view any of these
bestsellers by clicking on the live link in the title. Most
titles are published in paperback and as an ebook.
Paperbacks are available in traditional bookshops. Both
print and ebook formats are available online.

Find more titles and sign up to our readers' newsletter at
http://www.johnhuntpublishing.com/paganism
Follow us on Facebook at
https://www.facebook.com/MoonBooks
and Twitter at https://twitter.com/MoonBooksJHP